Student to Scholar

Student to Scholar

The Guide for Doctoral Students

Robert E. Levasseur, Ph.D.

MindFire Press
Annapolis, Maryland

ISBN–13: 978–0–9789930–2–3
ISBN–10: 0–9789930–2–0

Library of Congress Control Number: 2006908869

Published by MindFire Press of Annapolis, Maryland
(www.mindfirepress.com)

"The mind is a fire to be kindled,
not a vessel to be filled."

Plutarch

Table of Contents

A Personal Note from Dr. L

If you are currently a doctoral student or expect to be one soon, and you want to get the most out of the time and money you invest in your program of study, this book is for you.

As a working adult who recently completed his Ph.D. and is now a full-time faculty member at a major online university, I know what you are or will shortly be going through. As someone who earned his degree in the shortest allowable time, I also have some ideas that I believe can help you to maximize the learning from your program while minimizing the time invested in obtaining your degree.

Because I have blazed my own trail and am currently helping others do the same thing, I know quite a bit about the problems, wants, and needs of students, particularly Ph.D. students pursuing a degree in an online environment. And since you and so many other people are pursuing or seriously considering the pursuit of a higher degree, I felt it was imperative to share some of my knowledge.

You see, I am a firm believer in the power of people to make a difference in the world. At the university from which I earned my Ph.D., they call it "effecting positive social change" and they refer to it as having "a higher purpose." I like these phrases because they capture the self-actualizing goals that so many doctoral students share.

Of course, we all want to make more money and live better lives as a result of earning this capstone degree, but also characteristic of most doctoral students is the desire to give something back—to honor and repay, directly or indirectly, the wonderful people who have encouraged, loved, and supported them as they pursued their dream.

With the goal of assisting you in your unique quest for the doctorate, I offer you in this book some ideas to facilitate your transition from a being a good student to being a great scholar, the most important academic transition you will ever make.

As a student, you received guidance from your instructors in the form of assigned texts, required readings, specific home work assignments, and bounded term papers. To become a scholar, you must learn (a) how to identify what to read, (b) how to read critically what you find, (c) how to design your own research projects to add to our collective store of knowledge, and (d) how to report your findings to a community of scholars.

The ideas incorporated in this book include insights into what it means to be a doctor of philosophy, what you, as a student, have to learn and demonstrate to obtain your degree, and how you can go about making your doctoral goal a reality in the most expeditious, positive, learning-filled way possible.

I hope you enjoy the journey!

Chapter 1

The Evolving Role of the Doctorate

The Ph.D. is a research degree. A doctor of philosophy is, by definition, a lover of wisdom. In practice, the primary historical function of the doctor, particularly the doctor of philosophy, has been to discover and disseminate new knowledge.

The doctor/professor accomplished this by teaching others and by applying this new knowledge to the solution of real world problems. Until recently, these three roles, discovery, teaching, and application, have been the focus of the professoriate.

Ernest Boyer, in his groundbreaking book *Scholarship Reconsidered*, made a convincing case for the emerging and increasingly essential role of integrating existing knowledge as the fourth responsibility of the doctor of philosophy.

> By integration, we mean making connections across the disciplines, placing the specialties in a larger context, illuminating data in a revealing way.... Those engaged in discovery ask, "What is to be known, what is yet to be found?" Those engaged in integration ask, "What do the findings mean?" Is it possible to provide a larger, more comprehensive understanding? (Boyer, 1990, pp. 18–19)

Thus did Boyer legitimize the role of the doctor as an integrator of existing knowledge in new and powerful ways; ways that today's complex personal, team, organizational, and social problems require.

To summarize, the primary roles of a modern doctor of philosophy are the discovery, integration, teaching, and application of new knowledge. I personally find this broad responsibility both challenging and exciting.

Chapter 2

Speed vs. Quality

When I was a doctoral student, my mentor was a terrific fellow who had very high academic standards (which I appreciated), but who was also blessed with a sense of humor (which I also appreciated).

A short time into my program of study, he correctly surmised that I had several key goals: (a) to learn as much as possible by doing high quality work, (b) to save money by finishing as quickly as possible, and (c) not to trade-off one (quality) for the other (speed).

In short, I wanted it all. Compromise was not an option. Given this set of specifications, my mentor came up with a saying that became my mantra: "Work hard, go fast, save money!"

Using the concepts explained in this book, I earned my degree in the minimum amount of time permitted by my university, which was 55% of the time it takes the average student at my university to complete his or her doctorate.

In addition, my level of scholarship was high enough to earn me a full-time position on the faculty, where every day I have the opportunity to help others achieve their goal of earning a Ph.D. Needless to say, this is a dream come true for me.

Now, it is time to work on making your dreams come true by explaining some of the concepts, methods, tools, and techniques that I used to accelerate my doctoral program dramatically. We start, in the next section, with the extremely important notion of the connection between quality and speed.

The Quality-Speed Connection

What is the relationship between working fast (speed) and doing good work (quality)? How do they interact to affect the time it takes to complete your program (i.e., completion time)?

The following constitutes the conventional wisdom on the subject:

- Focusing on speed decreases quality.
- Focusing on quality decreases speed.
- Therefore, to maintain quality you have to go slowly, which increases time to completion.
- Alternatively, to maintain a high speed and complete your program expeditiously you have to sacrifice quality.

If you believe that speed and quality work at cross purposes and you act accordingly, they will appear to work against each other. In short, if you are not careful, you will join the ranks of doctoral students who have made this a self-fulfilling prophecy.

Please understand that viewing the world in this way is not per se a bad thing. I know people who started their programs when I did and took as long, or longer, than the average student (at least twice as much time as me) to earn their degrees because they placed a premium on learning and relegated completion time to secondary status.

There is absolutely nothing wrong with this approach. It suited their needs perfectly. In fact, if they had tried to act like me, they would not have had the doctoral experience they were seeking.

I know others, thankfully only a very few, who just wanted a piece of paper. To them, speed was of the essence, while quality (i.e., learning) did not matter. Fortunately for me and the majority of hard working students who want their degree to mean something, these substandard students became the focus of much faculty attention.

This meant that they had to revise their work substantially so that it at least met the minimum quality standards of the university. In the end, the few who did succeed in earning a doctorate by taking this low-quality path failed to shorten their programs of study. If anything, they lengthened them.

So, assuming that optimizing both quality and speed is as important to you as it was to me, let us continue.

By now, you may have begun to figure out the secret to accelerating a doctoral program. It involves understanding the relationship between quality (and speed), and a key hidden variable that lies at the center of the process—revision time.

The Secret to Accelerating Your Journey

This is the doctoral optimizing secret:

    A. To accelerate your doctoral journey, focus on minimizing revision time.

    B. To minimize revision time, do your work right the first time.

    C. To do your work right the first time:

        1. Begin your dissertation on day 1.
        2. Stand on the shoulders of giants.
        3. Think, read, research, and write like a scholar.
        4. Practice the 4 Ps every day.

If you follow this advice, you will learn a great deal during your journey, become increasingly adept at demonstrating what you learn in the form of high quality work products and publications, and move faster and with greater ease and peace of mind toward your ultimate goal.

Important Clarification

Let me make it very clear that the name of the game in doctoral work is revision. Revision is inevitable since, as a practical matter, no one gets it EXACTLY right the

first time, whether the "it" is a 10 page learning agreement for a major paper, the 100-plus page, in-depth,
scholarly paper itself, or a 200-hundred-plus page
doctoral dissertation.

So, try your best to get it right the first time, but be
prepared to revise your work based on the feedback you
receive from those assigned to read it critically (like
instructors, assessors, and dissertation committee
members); and apply the guidelines described in this
book to help you minimize your revision time and, in
turn, your degree completion time.

Chapter 3

Four Ways to Accelerate Your Program

Begin your dissertation on day 1.

Traditional thinking says that you should start by studying your field (e.g., management, psychology, education) and then, when and only when you are ready, embark on your dissertation work. In practice, this leads to a more or less linear process of course work, completion of major papers, and the dissertation.

While there is nothing inherently wrong with this linear notion, you must not follow it strictly if you want to accelerate your program. Here are some of the drawbacks of the traditional approach:

- First, it permits you to languish in student mode while harboring the misconception that you are becoming a scholar. In fact, taking classes gives you more practice at being a student, something with which you are already quite familiar, but very little practice in your new role of scholar.

- Second, it encourages you to study for study's sake, which could disconnect what you study in the early phases of your program from work on your dissertation. This would inevitably and unnecessarily extend your degree completion time.

- Third, it leaves all of the important work of identifying a topic for your dissertation that is both researchable and doable, which is a very complex problem solving process, until the latter stages of your program when you are fatigued from your doctoral journey and under pressure to complete the process. These factors make it that much harder and more stressful to solve the mystery of what to do for your dissertation research.

If not in the traditional linear fashion, then how should you approach your dissertation? The answer is simple: start thinking about your dissertation research at the very beginning of your doctoral program.

A little later, when we discuss the dissertation as a major deliverable of your program, we will go into some depth about how to link your ideas about broad problem areas you might want to study to existing research to enable you to find a doable, researchable project.

For now, let us focus on the broader issue of why you should begin your dissertation research on day 1 of your program:

- First, you replace a more scattered view of your program, which doing course work in a variety of subjects inevitably engenders, with a more purposeful, funnel-like focus. Focusing on a specific, albeit very tentative, dissertation topic enables you to customize much of your course work and more of your major papers so that they inform and support your dissertation topic. As a result, you still benefit from learning the material in each course and paper, but you also work toward a clearer conception of the theories, research, and professional practices that relate directly to your area of interest for the dissertation.

- Second, the process of identifying a researchable dissertation project requires you to learn and to apply many of the higher-order doctoral skills that differentiate the scholar from the student.

- Third, because this process requires you to act like a scholar, it makes you a better student and, thereby, enables you to do higher quality work and learn more in your courses and from working on your major papers. This will accelerate the preparatory stages of your program.

- Fourth, by making you a better scholar before you reach the dissertation stage, this approach accelerates the dissertation stage as well.

- Fifth, the net result of beginning your dissertation on day 1 is to shorten program completion time (by shortening both the preparatory stages and the actual dissertation stage) and to increase the quality of your work.

Two Caveats

First, don't assume that your mentor will encourage you to think in this non-traditional, iterative way. If so, fine. If not, keep working on your ideas for a dissertation topic by yourself, but don't involve your mentor actively in the process until he or she is ready to work with you (probably much later in your program).

This is both the right and the respectful thing to do. There are, after all, always other non-traditional, iterative thinkers (i.e., students, administrators, other faculty, and alumni) to discuss your preliminary ideas with if your mentor is not amenable.

Second, do not try to make everything you study in the early phases of your program serve the purpose of your tentative dissertation topic. After all, your topic may and probably will change many times before you finally settle on a doable, researchable one, get it approved, and complete your dissertation research.

Use your tentative topic to help you give focus to your program, but don't let it become a straitjacket. Realize that you will have to do many assignments that have no connection to anything as specific as a dissertation topic. They are necessary to teach you important things about your field of study (such as its primary theories, research findings, and practices) or skills that you will need to do independent, scholarly research (such as critical thinking, analysis, and writing).

The bottom line is to use your common sense. If an assignment gives you the option of working on something related to your ultimate dissertation topic, do it for all of the reasons mentioned above. Otherwise, do the assignment as specified to the very best of your ability, without gerrymandering it to fit your perceived need to work on your doctoral topic, and move on.

Stand on the shoulders of giants.

In a letter to a fellow scientist, Isaac Newton said, "If I have seen further it is by standing on the shoulders of giants." As a scholar, it is your responsibility to do the same thing.

In practice, this means that you must search the literature of your field for prior knowledge about your topic of interest and use it to inform your work. The sources of this existing knowledge include, but are not limited to, (a) books by leading theorists, (b) articles published by prominent researchers in refereed journals, (c) dissertations, (d) reports, (e) descriptions in popular publications of real world applications, and, of course, (f) information available via the Internet.

Identifying, critically analyzing, and building on the work of other scholars "grounds" your work. In a sense, you plant your seeds in the ground prepared by your scholarly predecessors. As an example, consider that many contemporary theories of change management essentially follow an unfreezing-movement-refreezing format. They are grounded in (i.e., stem from) the work of Kurt Lewin, the great, twentieth century humanistic psychologist, who developed the basic concepts of force field analysis, action research, group dynamics, and change management.

How, you ask, does grounding your work accelerate your doctoral program?

First, it shows your professors that you are a student who is serious about becoming a scholar. Second, it elevates your work to the level required of a doctoral student. Third, as a result, it dramatically shortens revision times. Finally, since all post-doctoral, scholarly work is grounded in the literature, it provides valuable practice at developing an essential doctoral skill; one, I might add, that you will have to demonstrate in your dissertation to graduate.

As a teacher, I can say without hesitation that one of the ways in which I can tell which students will become the best scholars is how well they ground their work.

The best of them support every major assertion they make, whether in an assignment, a posting to an online discussion forum, or a major paper, with a reference to the appropriate literature. Furthermore, they use an in-text citation that is in correct APA style (many universities use the American Psychological Association style manual as their standard).

A typical student posting might look something like this:

> I think that action research is a useful change management technique.

In contrast, a budding scholar might post something like this:

Many change management experts use the action research method (Burke, 1987).

For educational purposes, let us spend a few minutes comparing (i.e., how they are alike) and contrasting (i.e., how they differ) these two statements along a number of dimensions, including the general tone, person, voice, and style of each posting.

Dimension	Student	Scholar
Tone	Familiar	Professional
Person	First	Third
Voice	Active	Active
Style	Personal	APA

In the first posting, the student writes in a familiar, conversational tone (e.g., in the first person). In the second posting, which is preferable at the doctoral level, the scholar conveys the same information in a much more professional tone (e.g., in the third person).

Note very carefully that both people use the active voice (i.e., the sentences follow a subject-predicate-object format). It is a myth that good doctoral writing is in the passive voice. All writers should strive to write in the active voice. Use the spell checking feature of your word processor to help you find and eliminate sentences in the passive voice.

To help you appreciate the power that the active voice gives to your writing, here are several examples of the same sentence written in the active and passive voice.

Compare them and see if you don't agree with me that the active voice is preferable.

Active Voice

> Many change management experts use the action research method (Burke, 1987).

Passive Voice

> The action research method has been used often by change management experts (Burke, 1987).
>
> The frequent use of action research by change management experts has been documented (Burke, 1987).

Whether you choose to write in the active or passive voice, grounding your work in the literature will enable you to distinguish your work from that of others and will result in it being of higher quality the first time. As you know already, this will decrease revision time.

When aggregated over the totality of your doctoral work, this has the potential to significantly shorten your program completion time. So, strive to ground your work from the beginning (in ways we will discuss a little later) and you will do higher quality work and accelerate your doctoral program.

Act like a scholar.

If you want to become a scholar, then you need to act like one. As a student undergoing a metamorphosis into a scholar, you need to learn how to think, search, read, research, and write like a doctor of philosophy. In fact, before your university confers a Ph.D. on you, you will have to demonstrate that you can apply these doctoral level skills in an acceptable manner to complete your dissertation.

You acquire and demonstrate these higher-order skills throughout and as a result of your doctoral program, but (as it was put to me by a wise former professor) your ultimate goal and challenge, as encapsulated in the dissertation (which is the "final exam" of your doctoral program), is to demonstrate to your committee and, thereby, your peers in the academic community that you can "design, conduct, and report the findings of a research project."

The moral of the story is clear. The race and the prize (Ph.D.) go to those who master these fundamental doctoral skills early on. Much of the rest of the book will focus on how to acquire these essential competencies, but for now suffice it to say that the early mastery of these tools of the doctoral trade is an essential mechanism for accelerating your doctoral journey.

Practice the 4 Ps.

No, I am not referring to the 4 Ps of marketing (i.e., Product, Price, Promotion, and Place). The 4 Ps of doctoral study are:

- Planning
- Persistence
- Patience
- Participation

Planning

To complete your program in record time, you must have a plan. Not a detailed plan, since it is nearly impossible to predict when you will encounter obstacles on the road to the doctorate, but a broad plan with an overarching vision, a tentative dissertation focus, a rationale for how each major element of your program will contribute to your learning (in general) and your dissertation (in particular), and a timeline for the completion of these major elements.

Make sure that your overarching vision incorporates your goals, such as your desire to learn a lot, do high quality work, and complete your program expeditiously. This vision is your target, your magnet, your guiding force. Make it compelling. Make sure it speaks to all of your wishes, hopes, and dreams.

Persistence

As a former president of the university I received my Ph.D. from was fond of saying, you should expect to hit an occasional "bump in the road" on your way to the doctorate. When it happens, deal with it and move on.

Bumps in the road can take an infinite variety of forms. Troubles ironing out administrative issues, problems with your laptop, adjusting to the type and level of work required in a doctoral program, balancing the demands of an already full life with the requirements of your program, death in the family, personal injury or illness; the list goes on and on.

So, expect to hit a few bumps (even though you can't predict what form they will take or when they will occur) and, when you hit one, do everything you can to not let it derail your efforts.

The alternative, which is to build each one into something larger than life, makes them seem more like roadblocks than bumps, and drains precious energy that you will need to conserve to help you meet the demands of your program.

I can't tell you how often this sage piece of advice came to my aid as I encountered my unique set of challenges on the road to the Ph.D. Just one personal anecdote will illustrate how I used this philosophy to my advantage.

When I was in the dissertation phase of my program, I considered either (a) doing an in-depth case study in a client company or (b) performing an experiment involving the management students in a school where I had taught part time for a long time. As I developed the research design for each alternative, the high quality of the two options I had for conducting my dissertation research project struck me. Was this not too good to be true?

Yes, of course, it was. Before I could home in on either option, a university in the Caribbean offered me a full-time teaching position. As they say, it was a tough job, but somebody had to do it. So, with my wife's whole-hearted support, I accepted; and poof, just like that, my dissertation research options went up in smoke.

Needless to say, while I was delighted to have achieved my goal of being a full-time professor of management (which was the primary reason why I, a working adult, went back to school to earn my Ph.D.), I was not pleased to lose both of my dissertation research options as a result. However, with the wise advice of my former university president about bumps in the road ringing in my head, I decided to just move on.

To my great surprise, happiness, and relief, I soon discovered a completely different way to do a study in my area of interest (i.e., leadership and organizational change). It consisted of using a statistical methodology called meta-analysis to do an aggregate analysis of the findings of existing, published, quantitative, primary research studies that had previously sought answers to the questions I wanted to study in my own dissertation research. Since all of the studies I needed for my dissertation research were already published and available via online databases, my problem of finding a doable, researchable dissertation topic went away.

In no time, I was back on my time line and working steadily toward my goal. As you already know, I made it on time.

The move to the Caribbean, which as you can imagine was a life-changing event, and many other, smaller events along the way to my doctorate, proved to me again and again the virtue of being persistent. I urge you to be equally persistent in your quest. It will pay off.

Patience

Whoever said that patience is a virtue, knew what he or she was talking about. Although I have always been a considerate person, patience has never been my strong suit. Ironically, I am more patient today than ever due to the numerous opportunities to practice presented to me during the course of my doctoral studies.

Within the context of your doctoral program, I believe that you will get farther faster if you assume that people are doing their best and are really interested in helping you to resolve your burning issues (i.e., bumps in the road), than if you assume the opposite.

Doctoral work is hard and takes considerable time to do right. So why is it that some students expect assigned readers to review assignments or major papers that took them days, weeks, or even months to complete practically overnight?

As a student, I tried to see things from the point of view of others, such as the faculty, staff, and administration, as well as my own. As a faculty member, I try to do the same thing. When I succeed, I generally find that being patient is not so hard.

On the interpersonal side, being as considerate and patient as possible when making requests of others is more likely, as you know, to engender a timely, helpful response than going immediately on the offensive. People, for some reason, just don't respond well to threats.

So, even though you are paying for your education and, as a result, are entitled to people's consideration, you need to realize that you are not the only one making demands on their time. Be patient and polite, and you will expedite the solution of any obstacles (i.e., bumps in the road) that might otherwise delay your progress toward the degree.

Besides exercising patience with others, it is important to be patient with yourself. Doctoral work is tough. So, cut yourself some slack from time to time. It will help you to stay motivated and on track.

Participation

A doctoral journey is a very special ride; one that you will want to experience to the fullest. So, by all means, participate. Share your thoughts, experiences, and questions with others. Listen attentively to their views. You may never have the chance to engage in such a learner-centered dialogue with other inquisitive minds about important ideas that really matter to you.

By being yourself and interacting often with others in your program, you make a major contribution to the development of the learning community (community of scholars) that you collectively represent. Others benefit from your active and considerate participation and your unique perspective; and vice versa.

As a valued and respected member of the community, you, in turn, benefit from the individual and collective intelligence of your colleagues. As a new student, you will ask for and receive from more advanced students (a) inside information on program requirements from people who have taken the courses and written the papers you are going to have to deliver, (b) the inside story on the faculty, and (c) insights into a host of other specific issues that matter to you. Of course, when you become an advanced student/scholar, you will have and should embrace the opportunity to share the wisdom you have accumulated with new students.

Inside information can really help you to accelerate your program. Consider, for example, the benefit of knowing that a certain faculty member, although a stalwart in his or her field of study, does not respond to student questions in a timely manner or doesn't provide helpful, detailed feedback on student work. Or, the benefit of knowing how much and what type of work is really involved in that required statistics course.

In short, to get answers to questions that can really help shorten your program, or at the very least make it less taxing, go out of your way to meet and interact actively and considerately with the members of your community. Don't be a hermit. It is counter-productive, and it will lengthen your program completion time.

Conclusion

So far we have examined a number of important generic issues related to your doctoral program, such as the role of the Ph.D., the myth of speed versus quality, and four major ways to accelerate a doctoral program.

Now, we turn our attention to the specifics of how to accelerate your program by (a) acquiring the higher-order thinking, searching, reading, and writing skills required of a scholar and (b) applying them to several of your major program deliverables.

Chapter 4

Higher-order Doctoral Skills

Critical Thinking

What does it mean to exercise critical thinking? Does it mean to be negative and adversarial? Does it mean to provide constructive criticism? Or does in mean something totally different? To explore the nature of critical thinking, we begin by examining the concept of left and right brain thinking.

Left and Right Brain Thinking

Brain research suggests that the left and right sides of the brain have distinct and complementary functions. Simply put, the left brain is the seat of logic and, hence, analytical thinking, and the right brain is the seat of intuition and, hence, system thinking.

So, is critical thinking left-brained, analytical thinking, or is it right-brained, system thinking? Perhaps by examining the thinking of a few great scholars we can answer this important question.

Everyone knows that Einstein was one of the great minds of all time. Clearly, Einstein's theory of relativity qualifies him as a left-brained, analytical person.

Leonardo Da Vinci, as the painter of the Mona Lisa and The Last Supper, clearly qualifies as one of the great creative thinkers of all time, a truly right-brained, artistic, systemic person.

But, wait a minute you say. Wasn't Einstein also a concert-level violinist and Da Vinci also a brilliant inventor and the chief engineer of the Duke of Milan?

Apparently, the great thinkers were really both left and right brained; that is, whole-brained. When confronted with a complex problem, they first used their right brain to get the big picture, systemic view of it; then they used their left brain to break it into manageable subproblems which they analyzed for insight into the solution of the original problem. And so on and so forth.

As we have seen, the alternating use of the left and right sides of the brain, called whole-brain thinking, is the hallmark of great thinkers. So, if it is to embody the high level thinking exemplified by great minds, our concept of critical thinking must incorporate whole-brain thinking.

Lower vs. Higher-order Thinking

To differentiate the work of students from scholars, academics use a framework called Bloom's Taxonomy. According to Benjamin Bloom, there are multiple levels of thinking. They follow a hierarchy from the lowest to the highest order or level:

- Knowledge
- Comprehension
- Application

- Analysis
- Synthesis
- Evaluation

Students tend to focus on the lower level skills since the educational system at the levels below the doctorate tend to emphasize their use. For example, in the early grades you learned by memorizing certain facts, such as "Columbus sailed the ocean blue in 1492." By regurgitating these important facts on command, you demonstrated your knowledge.

As you progressed to the middle grades, teachers asked you to think at a higher level. For example, upon correctly stating in science class that the earth is round, not flat, a good teacher might have asked you a follow-up question about how you knew the earth was not flat. Being a good student, you might have answered that the sun rises and falls every day, which would not happen if the earth were flat. This would have demonstrated your comprehension of the basic concept.

At some point in your educational progression, a teacher undoubtedly asked you to illustrate still higher-order thinking, perhaps on a test, by applying what you knew and understood to the solution of a problem. For example, she/he might have said, "If the earth is round and rotates counter-clockwise on its axis, and it is noon time where we are in New York City, is it morning or afternoon in Los Angeles?"

Knowledge, comprehension, and application are important at any educational level, including the doctoral level. However, in addition to these lower-level skills, you will need to demonstrate the higher-order thinking implicit in analysis, synthesis, and evaluation in your doctoral work.

Continuing the illustration, imagine a college professor asking you to write a term paper analyzing the musical styles of several composers. You paper would certainly have presented some basic, descriptive information on their styles (to demonstrate both your knowledge and comprehension), and an example or two of each style (as applications of their musical theories).

But, at this level, you would have had to demonstrate a still higher level of thinking. So, your paper would have included a substantive section in which you compared and contrasted the commonalities and differences, respectively, in the styles of the composers. This would have constituted the primary demonstration of your critical thinking about the composer's musical styles.

For your final exam in an MBA class on OB (Organizational Behavior), a professor might have upped the intellectual ante by asking you to synthesize into a coherent theory of human motivation the theories of Lewin, Maslow, McGregor, and one other humanistic psychologist of your choice.

Finally, for a major paper in your doctoral program, your might have to evaluate critically the ideas of four to six eminent human development theorists, such as Freud, Erikson, Jung, and Maslow. This assessment would require that you demonstrate all six levels of thinking, especially the higher-order ones, listed in Bloom's Taxonomy.

When faced with this assignment, an ordinary doctoral student would probably write a paper that described the works of the individual theorists in great detail and, in a short concluding section, compared their views on one of more issues representing the focus or theme of the paper.

A budding scholar on the other hand, would clearly identify a central, organizing theme for his or her essay and build the entire paper around this theme. Rather than focusing on the theorists ideas in isolation and tying them loosely together at the end, as the student would likely do, the scholar would use the ideas and arguments of the theorists to illustrate, illuminate, and inform various aspects of the central theme.

The difference between the scholarly essay and the typical student essay would be, to paraphrase Mark Twain, like the difference between lightning and the lightning bug.

Later on we will examine some specific examples of good (i.e., scholarly) doctoral writing. But for now, we will continue with our discussion of critical thinking.

So, what is critical thinking?

Is critical thinking whole-brain thinking? Or, is critical thinking higher-order thinking? In practice, it is both.

As a doctoral student, your work must reflect all levels of thinking, particularly the higher-order thinking skills of analysis, synthesis, and evaluation. In addition, your work should incorporate a whole-brain approach that uses right-brained, systemic thinking to support left-brained, analytical thinking, and vice-versa.

Critical Reading

Scholars must know how to read critically. This means that, from this point on in your doctoral program, you must learn to apply your critical thinking skills to everything you read. It is no longer sufficient to read for knowledge, comprehension, and application. You must also analyze, synthesize, integrate, and evaluate what you read.

Okay, you say, "I buy it, but how do I do it?

Before answering this question, I want to make one very, very important point about what you must read as a doctoral student.

Read the Original Works

A colleague of mine describes what we as professors expect of doctoral students in this way. As an undergraduate or a masters' student, you read what others write about Adam Smith, Freud, Maslow, Piaget, and other important theorists. However, as a doctoral student you must read the original works (books, articles, etc.) by Adam Smith, Freud, and other major theorists and critically analyze them yourself.

The former, called secondary sources, include encyclopedias, web site overviews, textbooks, books by authors about the theorists and their work, and other documents not written by the theorists themselves. Read them for background material on the theorists you are studying.

The latter are primary sources written by the theorists (and researchers in the case of journal articles). You must read these original books and articles critically to understand, comprehend, apply, analyze, synthesize, and evaluate the ideas of the theorists (e.g., Freud and Maslow) and researchers yourself. This type of critical reading is the hallmark of the Ph.D.

Read With Your Whole Brain

There is no hard and fast formula for reading critically, but here is a method that has worked for me.

First, do a quick-and-dirty reading of major elements of the book or article (e.g., the abstract, table of contents, chapter summaries, and conclusions and recommendations) with the objective of developing an overall or big picture perspective of the work. Think of this as an intuitive, systemic view. What are the pieces and how do they combine into a coherent pattern or gestalt? What impressions are you left with from the initial reading? Keep it big picture; do it fast.

Second, do an in-depth, analytical reading of those sections of the work which contain the information you need to support your research objectives. Use Bloom's taxonomy to help you read at multiple levels and, thereby, apply both lower and higher level thinking to what you read.

In reading a journal article, for example, at the basic level read to know, understand, and be able to apply what the authors studied, how they studied it, what they learned, why they claim it is important, and what further research they recommend.

At the advanced level, analyze what the authors said about the problem, its significance, their research method, data analysis, findings, and the conclusions and recommendations for further study. Does what they say about each of these areas make sense to you as a researcher? If so, why? If not, why not? What criteria do you use to make this evaluation?

If this sounds straightforward, it really is. And, the best part is that you get better at it the more you practice. In short, by critically reading the critical thinking of other scholars, as incorporated in their books and articles, you become a better critical thinker yourself.

Critical Searching

Now that you know what you are supposed to read as a doctoral student and how you are supposed to read it, figuring out where to find it becomes the problem. Fortunately, information about any topic is only a click away if you own or have access to a computer. Because most doctoral students depend on a PC to do their work, I will assume that you have one as well.

If you have to write a major paper on the principles of human development, where do you begin your search for information? You can start with some facts and general information from web sites on the Internet and secondary sources (such as encyclopedia articles and textbooks) to get an overview of the field of study. However, as a critical thinker and reader, you now know that you must eventually discover and read the original books of major human development theorists as well as articles in refereed journals about research conducted on the subject.

The Process

The basic steps in the process of doing a literature review and writing about your subject are to:

1. Identify your sources.
2. Gauge their quality and applicability to your research.
3. Obtain your materials.
4. Read them critically.
5. Evaluate their quality and applicability.
6. Write your paper.

Note that this is inherently an iterative process, which means that you may need to retrace your steps from time to time. For example, if you discover the need for additional resources as a result of evaluating them or when writing your paper, then you will have to find and secure other source materials.

The Plan

Following this process, you decide to perform your search in two phases. In the first phase, you will search the World Wide Web for background or contextual material that will help you to understand more about human development, who the major theorists in the field of human development are, and what others say these theorists have said about the subject.

In the second phase, you will (a) obtain the original books by major theorists you intend to study and (b) access online databases to identify current and contemporary journal articles on a specific topic in the field of human development that you intend to study in depth in your paper.

For example, if you are interested in the effect of leadership style on the development of the members of an organization, you will choose different keywords for your online searches than if you are interested in how teaching style affects student development in middle school classrooms.

Phase 1--Secondary Sources

With your plan developed, you are ready to begin the first phase. Not knowing much about the subject, you decide to use the Google search engine to identify web sites with information about human development. So, you put the keyword "human development" in the box and click the search button. The result is literally, hundreds of millions of hits. Investigating the top 10 yields several interesting web sites and the name of a refereed journal, Human Development, which may have some pertinent articles.

Next, you decide to narrow your search. So you try "leadership and human development" and find much more interesting web sites, including some for books on leadership and human development that may serve as secondary sources for your paper, as well as sites that seem credible and provide the background material on human development that you were searching for.

With these ideas in hand, you next access a free, online encyclopedia, by entering the keywords "human development encyclopedia articles" or going directly to your favorite online encyclopedia, and read about human development. From this overview article, you identify a number of classical and contemporary theorists in the field, such as Freud, Erikson, Jung, Bronfenbrenner, Maslow, Hudson, and Kegan, and you make a list their important works that you intend to read and use in your paper.

At this point, you decide that you have enough general knowledge of the field of human development and its theorists, so you move on to the second phase of your search, the identification of those primary sources (i.e., original books, journal articles, etc.) that you will study carefully and use to support the arguments in your research paper.

Phase 2--Primary Sources (Books, Articles)

Having identified some of the original books by the major theorists that you intend to study in the first or theoretical foundations part of your paper on human development, your next task is to obtain them. If you have access to a college or university library, you can borrow them. Many of these research libraries are part of a larger library system, which may enable them to find copies of books you need through inter-library loan if they don't have them on their shelves.

Another approach, one which I used to accelerate my degree program, is to find the books on Amazon.com and purchase them used, rather than new, in most cases at a substantially reduced price. In this way, I was able to obtain the vast majority of the books I needed for my doctoral work quickly and inexpensively. Furthermore, I got to keep them in my library. Only the most arcane references were not available via Amazon, and in these few cases, I was happy to return the book to the library after I finished with it.

Your next step involves accessing online, scholarly databases in your field (which I am assuming you have access to as a result of being in a doctoral program), such as Academic Search Premier, Business Source Premier, ERIC, MEDLINE, PsycINFO, etc., for the purposes of identifying and obtaining relevant research literature on leadership and human development, the primary focus of the in depth portion of your paper.

Let's use Business Source Premier as the database, and find out what we can learn about our topic, leadership and human development, by accessing it.

Sometimes students follow a simple strategy of putting their keywords in individually when searching for articles. While this works, it generally produces too many irrelevant matches.

For example, performing a search for the keyword "leadership" yielded over 50,000 articles. Similarly, performing another search on the keyword "human development" yielded over 1500 articles. However, a search using the keyword "leadership and human development" yielded a much more manageable number, 25, all of which focus more directly on the impact of leadership on people development. This is, of course, what we set out to find.

By following this simple, two-phase search strategy, you can identify and obtain the source materials you need to ground your research paper. Caveat: It is very important to note that this is an example of how to do a scholarly search, not a blueprint. You should and will learn more about the process of finding, obtaining, and evaluating sources as you develop as a scholar. So, use this example as a starting point and engage your right brain to discover creative ways to improve your search effectiveness.

A Note on the Quality of Sources

Integral to the process of identifying resources for your work is the process of evaluating their quality as sources of information. This is basically a two step operation.

First, be aware when selecting your references that certain sources, such as web sites, are inherently of lower quality, as a rule, than published materials. However, not all published references are equal in quality. Magazine articles, for example, are subject to more editorial bias than are refereed journal articles, which must withstand a critical evaluation (i.e., peer review) by experts in the field. Similarly, the authors of books written for mass consumption, such as many popular best sellers, tend to base them less on scholarly research than on personal opinion and experience.

Second, when you obtain your reference materials, you must evaluate their quality for yourself. It is part of your responsibility as a scholar to do your own critical assessment of everything you read, from information on a web site to a theoretical argument by an important theorist to the findings of an important research study published in a prestigious journal. Never assume that what you access as reference material is of high quality. Always review it carefully and make up your own mind about its inherent quality and its applicability to your research.

Critical Writing

To write at the doctoral level, you must meet high standards of communication. Both the content of your writing (i.e., your ideas per se) and the formatting of your document (i.e., how you present your ideas) are equally important in doctoral writing. The areas that you must pay special attention to when you write are:

- Content
- Organization
- Grammar
- Style

Let us examine each in turn.

Content

Note that the focus in this chapter is on the general characteristics of doctoral writing. In later sections, we will examine the specific content requirements of some important deliverables in your doctoral program, such as major papers and the dissertation.

Reflect Higher-Order Thinking

First and foremost, your doctoral writing must reflect the higher-order thinking skills of analysis, synthesis, and evaluation. Book report style, descriptive writing that demonstrates lower-order thinking skills, such as knowledge, comprehension, and application, is not acceptable.

In short, your writing must demonstrate your ability to read and analyze the ideas of other scholars, evaluate them, synthesize or integrate them into a meaningful whole, if necessary, and use them in support of your own arguments. "He said, she said" content, which constitutes the bulk of undergraduate and masters level writing will not suffice at the doctoral level.

Get on the BOAT

Second, your writing must be balanced, objective, accurate, and tentative. By balanced I mean that you must present both sides of an argument, not just your point of view. Many new doctoral students have very strong opinions about things that matter to them, and, as a result, want to use their doctoral writing to "prove" that those ideas are right. While this is not a bad thing, it is also not a scientific or scholarly perspective.

Scholars know that such one-sided presentations are inherently biased. At the doctoral level, you must strive to present evidence for both sides of any position, and to demonstrate, by means of the work of other scholars and your own arguments, why your position is the stronger one.

Note the tentative nature of this last statement. This is intentional. In doctoral writing, you must reflect your basic understanding of the nature of scientific enquiry, that truth is subjective and, therefore, tentative. Early in our education, we learn about the nature of proof by experimentation, which is the hallmark of scientific investigation in the natural sciences. An object falls to earth when dropped, thus proving the existence of gravity. A chemical added to a liquid causes it to solidify, thus proving the validity of a chemical formula. It all sounds so objective and final.

As a doctoral student, you learn that proof is a much more tentative thing. For example, some people believe that the best leaders are take charge types who give orders and expect people to follow them. Others believe that the best leaders are charismatic ones who appeal to their followers' emotions and higher level needs and who give them wide latitude in figuring out how to get the job done.

Who is right? The correct answer is that it depends on the circumstances. If I were in a fire fight, I would want my lieutenant to take charge. But back in the office, I would prefer a manager with a more democratic style.

In short, one of the things that distinguish the writing of a student from a scholar is that a student knows he or she is right while a scholar knows he or she might be wrong.

Doctoral writers use evidence from the literature, not rhetoric, to support their contentions. Shouting louder, debating better, or otherwise hammering home the courage of your convictions is unacceptable in doctoral communication. Objective evidence, as opposed to subjective opinion, is the coin of the realm in doctoral work. Do you have real, preferably hard, data from scientifically conducted research that backs up your arguments? If not, then don't expect scholars to pay too much attention to what you have to say.

Accuracy and objectivity are closely related. In that regard, it is your responsibility to present the ideas of others from the literature as faithfully as you can, based on your own critical reading of their work. You must not distort their findings to make your point, even if you don't agree with those findings. Instead, you must present rational arguments for why an intelligent reader, in the situation you are dealing with, would find the arguments of those who stand with you more compelling than the arguments of those who stand against you.

Organization

Doctoral students get so involved in their research and writing and learn so much about the areas they study, that they often make the mistake of providing a great deal of information in a very condensed form without making the overall structure of their documents clear to an intelligent, but uninformed reader, and without providing clear transitions between parts of their work. This is not a good idea.

Instead, think of your readers as visitors to a National Park where you, the writer, work as a park ranger. The visitors, eager to explore the wonders of the park, do not expect you to accompany them on their journey, but they do expect you to provide them with a clearly marked trail map to help them navigate for themselves. So make sure that you have introductions and conclusions to each major section of your document and that you write smooth transitions in the middle that enable the reader to follow your train of thought easily. Also, provide headings (i.e., trail markers) to keep your readers from getting lost.

As in the next section, we are talking English 101 stuff here, nothing new or fancy.

Grammar

When it comes to grammar, there is no substitute for the fundamentals. Adhering to the tenets of Strunk and White's *The Elements of Style* or some other basic book of proper English grammar is a requirement of good doctoral writing.

Too often I read journal articles written by intelligent people that violate these basics, particularly when it comes to writing in the active voice. Sadly, students read these articles and erroneously infer that scholars are supposed to write in a stilted, old fashioned way. Nothing could be farther from the truth. In fact, the best writing—whether it is academic, professional, or personal— adheres to the rules of proper grammar.

I have had many doctoral students who were taken aback when informed that, at the doctoral level, the quality of their ideas (content) was not sufficient to overcome inferior formatting in the form of poor spelling, bad grammar, and incorrect APA reference citations and headings.

To these students, and others like them, I offer the following personal anecdote, which speaks directly to the need for both quality ideas and the expectation by true scholars of a quality presentation of those ideas.

A Grand Master's View of my Thesis

To satisfy the thesis requirements for my master of science in management degree, I chose to analyze marketing data and report my findings in what turned out to be a substantial paper. In this document, I went to great pains to demonstrate my newly acquired knowledge of marketing and statistical data analysis techniques, primarily regression analysis. I succeeded in doing this fairly easily to the satisfaction of my thesis advisor, a world-renowned scholar in the field of Operations Research.

However, to my surprise, he was not satisfied with my thesis. In fact, he asked me to meet with him at his home to discuss it.

At that meeting, we reviewed every single word in my thesis to determine the quality of my analysis and the quality of my writing. Since, he was pretty much convinced of the former, my thesis advisor concentrated on helping me to say precisely what I wanted to say in the best possible English. That meant, among other things, writing in the active voice exclusively, avoiding repetition, and choosing the right word to say what I really meant.

What an eye opener this was. One of the world's greatest experts in quantitative methods spent an entire afternoon of his valuable time working with me on the qualitative aspects of my thesis. Needless to say, this episode dispelled the myth of the scholar as a peddler of pompous, flowery, passive prose.

So, write in the strong, direct manner of a professional and people will happily read what you have to say. Adhere to a lesser, more amateurish standard and be prepared to spend considerable time revising your work to enhance its clarity and grammatical correctness.

Style

Class, panache, and flair are words that come immediately to mind when I think about style. However, we are talking about a different type of style here; namely APA (American Psychological Association) style.

The APA publication manual spells out in great detail the requirements one of the most frequently followed sets of guidelines for scholarly writing. Topics covered include the content and organization of a manuscript, grammar, bias in language, punctuation, spelling, capitalization, the use of italics and abbreviations, bibliographic and in-text reference citations.

You must adhere to the style guidelines specified by your institution, whether APA, Turabian, or some other, in all of your doctoral work.

For most students, learning APA is like learning a foreign language. While this is not necessarily an easy thing to do, you have no choice but to buckle down and learn APA style if you want to become a scholar. The sooner you do, the faster you will get through your doctoral program.

A Comment on Formatting

Every university has its own rules for formatting doctoral papers, particularly the dissertation. Like APA, these are non-negotiable. So the sooner you learn and apply them, the faster you will progress in your doctoral program.

Examples of the formatting requirements of one university are (a) using one, size-12 font throughout, (b) double spacing text, (c) indenting paragraphs by one-half inch, (d) not bolding or underlining, (e) using APA style headings, in-text citations, and bibliographic reference citations, and (f) writing in the third person exclusively. Be sure to enquire about the guidelines for your university and apply them from the outset.

Finding Your Voice

Before we conclude this section on critical writing, it is important to discuss how you as a student can express your opinions in a way that meets these guidelines and still allows readers to hear your voice. This becomes especially important to new doctoral students when they discover, sometimes to their chagrin, that they must write their major papers and dissertation exclusively in the third person.

That's right. Not only do you have to avoid the passive voice, but you also have to avoid the use of first and second person pronouns. That means that you can no longer simply say "I" think this or "you" should do that.

So, if a student or other writer cannot use the first or second person, how does a doctoral reader distinguish the ideas and research findings of other scholars from those of the writer?

In practice, this is not as difficult as students believe. The reason is that doctoral writers have to support their arguments with evidence from the literature, properly cited, to avoid charges of plagiarism. Anything not cited as the work of another is, by convention, ipso facto the work of the writer.

The following contrast between an improperly cited and a properly cited work will illustrate the difference. Keep in mind that the latter writing sample, while acceptable, does not necessarily represent the ideal.

Sample A [Unacceptable]

> Some say that money is a universal motivator. It is argued by others that it depends on the needs of the individual. I think the others are right, as I will explain in this essay.

Sample B [Acceptable]

> Some say that money is a universal motivator. Others argue that it depends on the needs of the individual (Maslow, 1954). In this essay, the author will critically evaluate the arguments for and against money as a universal motivator, and provide a rationale based on personal experience and empirical research evidence in support of Maslow's hierarchy-of-needs theory.

Note that the in-text reference citation (Maslow, 1954) refers to an original book by Abraham Maslow, *Motivation and Personality*. The correct, APA-style reference citation for this work is:

Maslow, A. (1954). *Motivation and personality*. New York: Harper and Row.

It is clear from Sample B that the writer intends to use one of the major works of Abraham Maslow as evidence to support his or her point of view (i.e., that money is not a universal motivator). This is not clear from Sample A.

In addition, the provision of an in-text reference citation in proper APA style not only clarifies and strengthens the writer's argument, it also gives credit where credit is due (i.e., to Maslow).

As a result, the reader is easily able to distinguish between the opinions of the writer (sentences one and three) and those of other scholars (sentence two).

Hence, the writer's voice emerges loudly and clearly and he or she avoids any hint of plagiarism.

Now, as an aside, note that the writer could make an even stronger case by citing in the first sentence the work of one or more published authors who believe that money is a universal motivator. Surely a little online research project could unearth several such useful references.

Finally, before moving on, note the clarity and power of the second sentence in Sample B, which is in the active voice, in comparison to the same sentence in Sample A, which is in the passive voice. This is why good writers strive to write exclusively in the active voice.

Conclusion

Having discussed the essentials of critical thinking and some general principles for applying them to doctoral researching, reading, and writing, it is time to move on to more specific aspects of the major deliverables that most doctoral students have in their programs. These include writing (a) learning agreements (contracts) for major papers, (b) the major papers themselves, and, of course, (c) the all important doctoral dissertation.

Chapter 5

Major Program Deliverables

Every doctoral student must demonstrate mastery of a domain of knowledge, such as leadership and organizational change, finance, or information systems. A significant element of this demonstration takes the form of written work, such as scholarly research papers, and, of course, the dissertation. In this chapter, we focus on the first of these major program deliverables. Our goal is to demystify the writing of research papers to a degree that will enable you to complete them more rapidly (at a higher speed) and effectively (with higher quality).

A Major Research Paper

Before a student embarks on the researching and writing of a major scholarly paper, he or she may have to write a contract or learning agreement which spells out in some detail the learning objectives for the study, specifies potential references or learning resources, and indicates how the student will demonstrate mastery of the knowledge area he or she plans to study.

The format of a learning contract follows the required structure and content of the major paper. One type of doctoral paper has a three part structure consisting of broad theory, current research in a field of study, and practical application of this theory and research to a professional problem. Since this is an excellent model for developing a scholarly research paper, one which you might opt to use whether you are required to in your program or not, we will examine it in some detail.

The first part of such a major paper is a review of the theories of important scholars in a given field of study, such as Freud and Maslow in human development. The second part is an exploration of the published research on a specific topic in that field of interest to the student, such as the impact of conflict versus cooperation in the workplace on employee performance and development. The third part is where the student applies the theories and research to a problem of professional importance, such as an evaluation of the training and development strategies employed by company XYZ in light of major theories and research in human development.

In effect, a good, scholarly research paper promises the reader (a) a review of the theoretical foundations of the study, (b) an in depth analysis of current and classic research on the primary theme or topic of the paper, and (c) a demonstration of how these theories and research findings are applicable in the real world.

In this context, a learning agreement is simply a roadmap of how you intend to go about constructing a scholarly research paper for your unique study. Here are some concrete suggestions for writing a focused, clear, integrated learning contract and the corresponding paper:

- Choose a single, coherent theme for the entire paper.

- Tie the theories, research, and practice to the theme.
- Use a funnel approach to integrate the parts of your paper.
- Follow the content and style guidelines provided by your school.

Central Theme

Choosing a central theme for your paper before you research or write it is an essential first step in the process. This theme is the mechanism that enables you to integrate your entire 100-plus page paper into a coherent, scholarly demonstration of knowledge. Without it, you may end up with a giant book report—an unconnected or, at best, loosely connected potpourri of theories, research findings, and professional practices—which is unacceptable at the doctoral level.

As a central theme for a paper on leadership, you might for example choose the effect of transformational leadership on an organization. This overarching theme would then inform your choice of theorists to include in the first or theoretical foundations section, articles for the current research section, and practical problem for the application section.

In this hypothetical case, James MacGregor Burns, who coined the term transforming leadership, would probably be among the theorists you would choose to study in your theoretical section. Articles by Bernard Bass, who conducted ground breaking research on what he called transformational leadership, would likely appear in your learning agreement research bibliography as potential learning resources. And, your application section might focus on leadership style and its effect on one or more organizations familiar to your.

Form Follows Function

In architecture, the function or intended use of a structure dictates its form. Thus, a circus enclosure, which must be easy to set up and tear down, becomes a tent, rather than a building. Likewise, the permanent home for a professional sports team, which must comfortably and safely seat tens of thousands of people, becomes a stadium, rather than a tent.

In the case of a major research paper and the learning agreement for it, this dictum requires you as a student to tie the theoretical, research, and practice parts of your paper directly to the theme, not vice versa.

This means that you must not study theories about one topic that interests you in the theory section, examine research about a second, unrelated topic that also interests you in the research section, and focus on practical issues concerning yet another unrelated topic in the application component. To do this would be to have your theme (three themes in this case) serve the theories, research, and practice, which is backwards and unacceptable.

Instead, what you must do is identify a topic or central theme and (a) develop a point of view for your paper, (b) outline the arguments you will make in your paper to explain your point of view, and (c) find evidence in the literature (i.e., theories for the first, research for the second, and examples of best practices for the third section) that support or refute (remember the need for balance in doctoral work) your arguments.

To clarify this process, it helps some students to think of it in terms of an analogy. Imagine that you are the moderator of a panel discussion among leading experts in the field. Hence, your role is to set the stage, ask the questions, facilitate the discussion, and summarize the results. Your role does not include acting like a member of the panel of experts.

In your capacity as moderator, you present a provocative, central theme for the discussion. Then, you ask each expert to comment on an aspect of that theme. When an expert makes an important point, you are careful to acknowledge it (which is the equivalent of providing in-text and bibliographic reference citations for each source in a research paper) before allowing another expert to present his or her point of view.

During the discussion, you encourage participants to examine ideas presented critically. After all of the panelists have weighed in on an issue, you compare (the similarities), contrast (the differences), evaluate what they have said, and attempt to synthesize the main points of the discussion into a coherent summary.

Applying this analogy to the structure of a major paper, imagine that you are the moderator for three separate panel discussions. In the first, the panel consists of distinguished theorists in the field, such as Sigmund Freud (on a human development panel) or James Mac-Gregor Burns (on a transformational leadership panel).

Your goal is to engage these eminent theorists in a spirited discussion about your central theme based on the theories they have put forth in their original books on the subject. To that end, you intentionally restrict your panel to major theorists. Secondary authors who have written books or text books about the ideas of your major theorists are not welcome on this panel of heavy weights.

Informed by the ideas presented and analyzed in this first panel discussion (the theory section), you moderate a second panel discussion among eminent researchers in the field, particularly those who have published articles in refereed journals. Once again, you restrict membership on the panel to esteemed scholars, such as Bernard Bass (on a transformational leadership panel).

Finally, you moderate a third panel in which you invite theorists, researchers, and practitioners to join you in a discussion of how to apply the theories and research findings gleaned from the first two panel discussions to an important problem in your area of professional practice.

Caveat: Keep in mind that this is just one way to create a major paper and the essential elements of a learning contract or agreement that describes it. You are under no obligation to follow this approach when outlining, researching, and writing your major papers and learning agreements.

The Magic Funnel

Think of a major paper as a funnel. At the top, it is wide. In the middle it narrows. And, at the spout, it is at its narrowest. The theoretical foundation section involves the broad explication of important theories in a field of knowledge that relate directly to a central theme. The more narrowly focused research section examines in detail current and, if necessary, classic research on a specific aspect of the field of knowledge that relates directly to the central theme. Finally, the application, which is even narrower, describes how these theories and research findings can illuminate and inform a single area of professional or organizational practice delineated by the central theme.

Follow the Guidelines

Every doctoral program is different. Therefore, the ideas presented above for fashioning major papers and their learning agreements may or may not be directly applicable to your situation. Hopefully, they will be. In any event, make sure that you follow the guidelines laid out by your school for each major paper you are required to submit. This will save you much revision time.

These guidelines typically cover both the content and formatting of your document. You must satisfy both of these essential requirements.

As I mentioned earlier, some doctoral students balk at having to follow precise guidelines for formatting of their papers. As a result, they spend many unnecessary hours revising their work until it meets the standards for doctoral work set by their university and enforced by its faculty.

The best advice I can give you is to buckle down and learn APA style, or whatever style your university requires, as soon as you can. If you find the manual hard to work with, obtain a guide book to APA that you like and use it for all but those special situations that require you to refer to the manual. For more on the topic of guides to APA, see the resources at the end of the book.

Note: If you are unsure about how to incorporate these content and formatting requirements into a major paper, check out the appendix at the end of the book. It contains an example of the theoretical foundations section of a major doctoral paper.

An Article Annotation

As part of a major paper, students sometimes have to demonstrate their ability to review a refereed journal article and critically analyze it. This is an exercise in critical thinking of the type described earlier in the discussion of higher-order doctoral skills.

If you must write annotations of this type, think of yourself as a (constructively) critical reviewer who is responsible for assessing the quality of the research described in the article and its applicability to your own doctoral work, particularly for your major papers and dissertation.

Each of your annotations must (a) include a reference citation in APA style, and must critically examine (b) the problem investigated, (c) the research method chosen by the authors to study the problem, (d) the findings of the study, (e) the contribution of the findings to knowledge in the field, and (f) the value of the article to you in your doctoral work.

It is not sufficient to describe the research and the findings and comment on their usefulness. You must put on your scholar's cap and evaluate (i.e., critically assess) aspects of the research like (a) the significance of the problem, (b) the pros and cons of the research method chosen, (c) how the researchers operationalized their variables, (d) the adequacy of the sample, (e) the reliability and validity of measurement instruments, (f) the level of statistical significance of the findings (if it was an empirical study), (g) the generalizability of the findings, (h) the overall quality, value, and applicability of the results to the profession and to your personal doctoral studies, and (i) any other aspects of the study that bear close examination. Furthermore, you must accomplish this in one or two tightly written pages.

Probably because they are still learning about them, students often fail to address adequately in their annotations the pros and cons of the research method used in a study. Since the Ph.D. is a research degree, it is essential that you develop and demonstrate your skill at doing this. The preceding paragraphs suggest some, but by no means all, of the dimensions of research methodology that you should examine.

Chapter 6

The Dissertation

In this section, we will examine several important aspects of the doctoral dissertation process by answering the following questions:

- What constitutes a quality dissertation?
- How do you turn a broad problem statement into a doable, researchable dissertation topic?
- How do you develop and implement a research focus?
- How can you design, conduct, and report the findings of a research project?
- How can you best manage the process and the key people in your program?
- What other aspects of the dissertation process do you need to know about to accelerate your program?

You are probably anxious to get answers to some of key these questions. So, let's get started.

What is a Quality Dissertation?

When I was a doctoral student, a very accomplished professor who had won several national honors for teaching excellence gave a seminar on how to write a quality dissertation. Although he was only expressing an opinion based on his personal experiences, what he said made a strong impression on me and, as a result, directly influenced my dissertation research.

He argued that every dissertation should make an original contribution. Replicating someone else's work would not be sufficient. This made sense to me, since the idea of the genius scientist hot on the trail of a new discovery was an idea that had been rattling around in my brain for some time, and, I might add, had been making me wonder if I had what it takes to earn a doctorate.

Fortunately for me and you, what my professor was talking about was placing your dissertation on a spectrum somewhere between "nothing original" on one end and "new discovery" on the other. You do not have to make an original discovery he argued, but you do have to do something original that distinguishes your work from the research of those who preceded you and whose shoulders you are attempting to stand on.

You might, for example, choose to do the same study as some one else, but select a sample from a different population. Or, you might decide to do an in depth qualitative study to explore the reasons underlying the quantitative findings of an earlier empirical study.

Similarly, you might choose to develop a survey based on prior qualitative, theory-building research to test several hypotheses put forth by the authors of the previous study. Perhaps you could add an additional variable to your study and perform a different type of data analysis, like regression analysis, to try to explain more of the uncertainty in previous findings. And so forth, and so on.

The point is that you should strive to do something original in your dissertation to make it unique. It is important to note, however, that you do not have to discover something new and extraordinary, like a cure for cancer, to complete a satisfactory dissertation. This revelation came as a great relief to me, because it made the dissertation seem doable by a mere mortal.

A second essential characteristic of a high quality dissertation, is that it make a difference in the world; however small. Why conduct natural or social science research if it doesn't have the potential to effect positive change? Therefore, you must ask yourself about the social significance of what you are doing. Who will benefit from what you hope to discover, and how will it benefit them?

While most dissertations are inherently beneficial to mankind, being explicit about the contribution of your work to humanity will (a) help ensure that is has some benefit, and (b) provide you with additional motivation to complete the research by tapping into your higher-level need for self-actualization.

So, what is a quality dissertation? Simply put, it is one that makes an original, however small, contribution to the advancement of our knowledge about the world.

To illustrate how these twin notions of (a) making an original contribution and (b) effecting positive social change can inform your dissertation research, consider my own dissertation studies.

I chose to do a meta-analysis of the effect of a trans-forming leadership style on follower performance and satisfaction (Levasseur, 2004).

Meta-analysis is a statistical technique for aggregating the findings of primary, empirical research studies conducted on a particular topic into a single, composite measure. In medical research, it might be an aggregate measure of the efficacy of a new drug, a new therapy, or a new surgical procedure. In my case, it was the impact of transforming (also known as charismatic, visionary, and transformational) leadership on follower perform-ance and job satisfaction.

The original contributions of my dissertation research included (a) the addition of five years worth of recent studies not incorporated in any previous meta-analyses, (b) the application of the latest meta-analytic methods, and (c) separate meta-analyses of experimental re-search findings versus those of correlational studies (based on surveys).

I compared the findings of a smaller number of avail-able experimental studies, which provided a stronger form of proof of the efficacy of transforming leadership, to those of the more prevalent correlational studies to determine if they supported the findings of the latter, which they did.

I believe that the world would be a better place if more leaders used the principles of transforming leadership whenever possible. In a fire fight, when there is no time to argue, I want my leader to be decisive and give effective orders. However, at work I prefer a more democratic style of leadership; one which engages people in a collaborative process of seeking better ways to do things.

Therefore,, in my dissertation research I set out to determine if the available empirical evidence, in the aggregate, supported the benefits of transforming leadership over traditional leadership, which it does. This was the social significance of my dissertation.

Choosing a Dissertation Topic

Many doctoral students are passionate about what they want to study, particularly in their dissertation research. This is a good thing, as it will sustain them through the long and rigorous dissertation process. However, as many discover to their chagrin, being passionate about a subject is not the only criterion for making it the focus of their dissertation research. Other factors, such as whether the proposed research is doable by a doctoral student and whether it is actually research, are equally important decision criteria.

Is it Doable?

This criterion is straightforward. It deals with whether or not you can conduct your research in a reasonable time frame with little or no outside help. After all, the dissertation is a demonstration of your ability to do research, not someone else's. Other than obtaining some technical assistance along the way from the likes of statisticians and editors, and then only if needed, you must conduct your own dissertation research. Within this broad constraint, you must decide on a reasonable time frame and whether a topic that may require a considerable extra investment of time (and tuition money) is worth pursuing or not.

Is it Research?

This criterion is a show stopper for some students, for reasons that the following examples will illustrate.

Work-related issues mesmerize certain students, especially professional people immersed in the solution of complicated organizational problems on a daily basis. Since their work often entails using sophisticated methods to solve these difficult problems, they view their projects as natural dissertation topics. Maybe they are, maybe they're not.

Say that your company is installing new software that promises to enhance the capabilities of the organization and, thereby, provide it with a competitive advantage. Your job is to evaluate the pros and cons of this new approach by conducting a pilot study and presenting its findings to management in the form of a written report.

Since your company is paying you to do this study anyway, it seems like you could kill the proverbial two birds with one stone if you could get your dissertation committee to allow you to make this your dissertation research project. Why might they not respond favorably to such a request?

While it is true that dissertation projects are exercises in complex problem solving, they are much more than that. In fact, the sine qua non of an acceptable doctoral dissertation study is that it promises to advance, even if only in a very small way, our accumulated store of knowledge as encapsulated in the literature on the subject.

So, before your committee, or more likely your dissertation chair at this preliminary point in the process, can approve your request to proceed, you will have to search the literature for evidence of prior research on your topic. This prior research is what will enable you to ground your work. If none exists, there is no frontier to advance and there are no shoulders to stand on. This makes your job (i.e., of gaining approval to do your work-related project as your dissertation study) much, much more difficult, since you now have to make a convincing argument for why research of this type is necessary even though no one else seems to think it is.

Don't get me wrong. Students do ground breaking research into new areas every day, but typically they are responding to bona fide niches or gaps in the knowledge encapsulated in the literature, not trying to make what is inherently a consulting project into a doctoral research project.

Since it is clear that a doctoral student with a passion for a topic determine must also ground it in the existing literature to make it the focus of his or her dissertation, the process for doing so ,which we will examine next, becomes extremely important. Before we do, however, let's take a minute to summarize the salient points made so far about how to choose a topic that will result in a quality dissertation.

In summary, the principal criteria for choosing a high quality dissertation topic are that you:

- Have a passion to study it.
- Believe that your findings will make a difference in the world.
- Believe that you can complete your study in a reasonable time.
- Have grounded it in the research literature.
- Believe that you can make an original contribution to the field.

Grounding Your Dissertation

When I was a doctoral student, I attended several seminars presented by authorities on the dissertation process. One of the aspects they emphasized most was translating one's initial passion for a broad problem area into a researchable dissertation topic. Needless to say, I found these sessions both illuminating and worthwhile.

The concept, as you know by now, is to find the giants whose broad shoulders you can stand on. This is both essential, as we have seen, and, while challenging, not too difficult to do in most cases.

Finding a dissertation topic and grounding it in the literature requires an iterative, three-step, trial-and-error process. These three steps are themselves the initial steps in a larger, iterative process for specifying the nature of your research project. The six steps in the research process are:

1. Define your broad problem area (Problem Statement).
2. Ground your dissertation research (Literature Search).
3. Specify the niche you intend to study (Purpose Statement).
4. Determine your goals (Research Questions or Hypotheses).
5. Specify your broad approach (Research Method).
6. Create your specific research plan (Research Design).

Let us examine each step briefly.

Broad Problem Statement

Start with a broad statement of the problem area you want to study, such as the importance of emotional intelligence to leadership effectiveness, the impact of post-Enron accounting regulations, the viability of business process reengineering, the results of "No Child Left Behind" on public education, or the reasons why mergers succeed or fail.

Focused Literature Search

Then, by means of online databases of scholarly journal articles or other library research methods, discover what other scholars have studied about your topic. For example, using the keyword "emotional intelligence" to search the Business Source Premier database yielded a list of 697 articles. Refining this search for the keywords "emotional intelligence" and "leadership" yielded a smaller, perhaps more promising, list of 190 articles.

Targeted Purpose Statement

Based on a review of the most promising articles discovered in the previous step, determine the aspects of your problem that previous researchers have studied, and how they have studied these areas, such as the research methods they have chosen, they way they have applied them, and to whom they have applied them. Pay particular attention to recommendations for further study.

Then decide what small, but significant, portion of that broad problem area you want to study in your doctoral research (and how) based on what you have discovered that other researchers have already done. By linking your proposed dissertation research in this fashion to that of your predecessors, you are effectively grounding your study in the literature. Your description of the targeted, grounded research project you propose to do is the purpose statement for your dissertation.

Early in your program, when you need only a rough idea of what you might study for your dissertation to help you tailor and, thereby, accelerate your program, completing the first three steps of this process will probably be sufficient. Later, however, you will need to complete the remaining three steps to sharpen the focus of your dissertation research.

Developing Your Research Focus

Imagine for the moment that you are in the end game of your doctoral program, the dissertation. Let us study the last three steps in the research process on the assumption that you have completed the first three and, as a result, have a specific, researchable, grounded topic in mind.

Research Questions/Hypotheses

What questions do you want to answer as a result of conducting your doctoral research? Do you want to know more than you have read in the literature on your topic about why business process engineering, mergers, educational policies, or anything else of interest to you works or doesn't work? Or are you more interested in knowing how strong the relationship is between two variables, such as emotional intelligence and leader effectiveness, or ethical behavior and profitability?

If you want to know the answers to "why" questions, then you may want to do some type of in-depth, qualitative (i.e., theory-building) research. On the other hand, if you want to know the answers to "how much" or "how strong" questions, you may to want to do some type of broad, quantitative (i.e., theory/hypothesis-testing) research. If you are interested in both types of questions, then you may want to do both in a mixed-method study that has both a qualitative (in-depth) and quantitative (empirical) component.

Although you may use research questions to guide any type of research study, it is customary to use research questions for qualitative studies and hypotheses for quantitative studies. Let us examine a few of each type before moving on.

A scholar interested in really knowing why mergers succeed or fail might ask the following research questions:

- Why do mergers succeed or fail?
- Do these reasons vary by industry?
- Do they vary by country?
- Do they vary by size of organization?

You get the picture, I'm sure. There are literally an infinite number of research questions that you might ask about any topic.

So, to make this discussion more realistic, imagine that you have decided to study mergers involving large, multinational companies. To that end you have selected two mergers involving a single firm—one a successful merger with another U.S. company, the other a failed merger with a European company. Your case study

research might then address the following central
questions:

- Why did the merger of XYX Corp, a large, multinational U.S. company, with another U.S.
  company succeed?
- Why did the merger of XYZ Corp, a large, multinational U.S. company, with a foreign company fail?
- What, if any, lessons emerge from this experience that might inform mergers of large, multinational U.S. companies with companies in the
  U.S. and abroad?

Knowing the questions you wanted to answer would
help you to choose specific research methods that would
maximize the likelihood of obtaining valid answers that
would generalize to the larger population. In this situation, since you wish to examine in depth two special
situations, a case study approach seems like it would
work best.

On the other end of the spectrum are quantitative
studies. In an empirical (i.e., measurement-focused)
study, you are trying to assess the validity of some
prior theory by testing the statistical significance of one
or more hypotheses derived from this theory using the
quantitative data collected for the purposes of the
study.

Say you found in a review of the existing literature a
theory that business process reengineering (BPR)
projects work better when the user groups participate

actively in the design effort, and you wanted to test that theory. You might then conceive of a study of the impact of user group participation (the independent variable in the study) on BPR project success (the dependent variable), and formulate the following null hypothesis (H_0) and alternative hypothesis (H_1) for testing by means of your study:

H_1: There is a positive correlation between user group participation and BPR project success.

H_0: User group participation does not affect BPR project success.

As we will discuss next, you would then choose a representative sample from your population of BPR projects, collect your data, and use it to test the validity of your alternative hypothesis.

Research Methods

Once you have selected a research paradigm for your dissertation research–qualitative (for theory building), quantitative (for theory testing), or mixed-method (for both), you must decide what specific research methods will yield the best results. There are numerous research methods, some of which you will have to study in depth as you approach the dissertation phase of your doctoral program. We will briefly describe several, along with their primary purposes.

The most popular qualitative research method is the case study. Most students are familiar with cases used in face-to-face and online classes for instructional purposes. However, when used as a research method, the case study has a very different purpose. According to Yin (2003), the goal of a case study is "to expand and generalize theories (analytic generalization) and not to enumerate frequencies (statistical generalization)" (p. 10).

Other qualitative methods are ethnography (used to study the culture of a group of people), phenomenology (used to study the essence of a common experience), grounded theory (used to develop a theory based on data), and action research (used in an iterative fashion to initiate changes, observe the effect of the changes, and make additional changes as required to improve the performance of a system.

Quantitative research methods fall into three main categories. The first is the classic experiment in which the researcher carefully selects test and control groups at random from a population, administers a treatment to the test group, measures the differences between the test and control groups, and statistically analyzes the differences to confirm or refute one or more hypotheses.

The second category involves the analysis of existing data. Typically, this takes the form of a quasi-experiment in which a change, either intentional or not, (a) has affected a subset of the population (not chosen at random) differently than the rest of the population, or (b) has affected all of the population in some way different from the past. In each case, it is possible to argue, although not as convincingly as for a true experiment, that the differences between the affected and unaffected segments of the population (in the first case) or between the population after versus before the change (in the second case) is a result of the change that took place.

For example, if the management of a firm believes that providing a new benefit, such as a shorter work week, flex-time, or job sharing, will motivate its workforce and lead to higher morale and performance, they may decide to make this new option available. By comparing the morale and performance of employees who opt for this new benefit to those who don't and the historical vs. current performance of those who do, the company can estimate the effectiveness of the new benefit.

Note: Another form of existing data analysis, which is a viable option for students who are good in mathematics, is meta-analysis. "Meta-analysis can be best understood as a form of survey research in which research reports, rather than people, are surveyed" (Lipsey & Wilson, 2001, p. 1). You may recall that I used meta-analysis in my own dissertation research.

Like experiments, the third category of quantitative methods involves the collection of new, primary data. However, unlike experiments, which obtain objective measurements, this category, called survey research, focuses on the collection and analysis of subjective data in the form of opinions self-reported in questionnaires by study participants. Everyone who has filled out a questionnaire is familiar with the variety of questions asked, from personal information to ratings of any number of factors on various scales.

When appropriately designed (i.e., to provide valid and reliable data), surveys provide data that is useful in testing the validity of hypotheses about the association (i.e., correlation) of variables. While evidence from survey research is not as inherently strong as evidence from experimental research, it is often the only way to get meaningful quantitative assessments of important (i.e., subjective) factors that researchers cannot otherwise measure, such as the effect of leadership style on employee job satisfaction.

Research Design

When you reach this stage in your research, you have answered the previous five questions in a way that directly informs the detailed design of your research project. You have articulated an important problem, grounded it in the literature, specified your purpose in studying it, chosen a research paradigm to help you answer your research questions or test your hypotheses about existing theories on the topic, and selected the research methods that you will use in your dissertation research.

Caveat: Because research design is a very large topic, we will focus on key aspects of the process here and leave a detailed study to you as part of your doctoral studies. In short, consider what follows to be helpful hints on how to design your research, not the definitive word on the process.

These are some of the key elements of research design:

- Research Methodology
- Ethical Considerations
- Variables and the Model
- Operationalizing the Constructs
- Validity and Reliability
- Population and Sample
- Data Collection and Analysis
- Presentation of Findings
- Iterative Nature of the Process

Research Methodology

Your research design is a blueprint for how you will conduct your dissertation research. This is both good and bad news. Bad news because it requires you to be very specific about how you are going to perform every aspect of your study, and good news in the sense that once completed it will serve as a roadmap for your journey.

Students often wonder how they will develop such a detailed plan without any prior research experience. Fortunately, there are specific, well-document, accepted methodologies for all of the research methods you might choose for your study, such as the previously mentioned Yin (2003) for case studies and Lipsey and Wilson (2001) for meta-analysis. In fact, you must select an appropriate methodology for your particular study, not make one up of you own, and defend that choice in your dissertation proposal.

Ethical Considerations

How you plan to treat participants in your study will be of great interest to your Institutional Review Board (IRB), the folks at your university who review and approve all research proposals. It should be of even greater importance to you, since it is your responsibility to ensure that you harm no one, physically or mentally, either intentionally or not in the conduct of your research.

Variables and the Model

Assume for a moment that you have decided to study the relationship between leadership style and follower performance. Your hypothesis is that the more collaborative the style, the higher the performance. In this case, the independent variable (X) is leadership style and the dependent variable (Y) is performance. You expect to find a positive correlation between X and Y. Hence, your underlying model is that $Y = f(X)$, where $f(X)$ means that Y is a function of (depends on) X.

You must make your variables and the relationships between them (i.e., the model) explicit and clear if you intend to do quantitative research.

Caveat: Each and every variable you include in your model places a burden on you to justify its inclusion in your study. This means providing a thorough review of the existing literature on it in your dissertation (the literature review). The time required to do this type of background work becomes a practical consideration, if not a limitation, in any dissertation research project.

What if you have chosen to conduct qualitative research, say into the phenomenon of the nurse-patient relationship? Since you are trying to develop a new theory, rather than trying to prove an existing one, the requirement to explicitly identify beforehand (a priori) the variables and their relationships (model) does not exist for qualitative research. In fact, the determination of those variables and, if possible, insights into their relationship(s) is the primary objective of qualitative research.

Caveat: Before you conclude that qualitative research is easier than quantitative research based on what I have said, I hasten to add that there is no scientific way to decide in advance whether a quantitative research project will be more difficult and time consuming than a quantitative one. Each has its own special challenges. In fact, the best way to decide which approach to take is to follow the six-step research process described in this section, not to choose (arbitrarily) a research method in advance.

Operationalizing the Constructs

If you are doing a quantitative study, you will have to decide how you are going to implement and measure each of the variables in your study. If, for example, you were a college professor and you decided to conduct an experiment to test the impact of leadership style on performance, then you might divide randomly selected, willing participants from your classes into two groups (test and control) for a simulation or role play in which each student performed the same task but under the direction of leaders exhibiting two very different styles (e.g., directive versus participative).

The exact specification of the directions for the task and the script and training of the leaders is part of the process of operationalizing your variables. As you can imagine, each researcher does this in the context of each empirical research project in a unique way.

Validity and Reliability

The validity and reliability of the research methods used in your study is of paramount importance. You must address both of these central concerns in your dissertation proposal in a manner convincing enough to get your committee to sign off on your research project.

There are two types of validity—internal and external. A study has internal validity if it measures what it intends to measure or, more generally, if it examines what it sets out to examine. In effect, a valid study gives real answers to the research questions, and/or provides a real test of the hypotheses.

As an example, consider the hypothetical leadership experiment, the goal of which is to measure the effect of leadership style on performance. Internal validity in this case deals with the extent to which the experiment actually measures the relationship between the two variables. When considering the research approach for this hypothetical situation, one can envision a number of threats to internal validity, including (a) the use of students in an academic setting as surrogates for employees working in an organization, (b) the relatively short duration of the experiment as compared to the ongoing nature of organizational leadership, and (c) the ability of students or even actors reading a script to simulate the effect of a real leader on followers. In your proposal, you will need to address how your study will avoid or mitigate relevant threats to internal validity such as these.

The other type of validity is external, which speaks to the degree to which the findings are generalizable to a larger population. In the case of our experiment on college students, a central question is to what extent the findings of the research apply to real leaders in real organizations. It is not impossible to make this case (many social science researchers have made similar arguments based on comparable research in the past), but if you want people to accept that your findings are applicable to a broader audience (i.e., as having validity external to your study) you must present a justification in your dissertation proposal for why this is so.

In the case of qualitative research, the external validity of the study may be harder to prove for different reasons. Researchers in most quantitative studies select a sample of participants randomly from a population. This selection ensures that the sample is representative of the larger population and, hence, that the findings of the research conducted on the sample are applicable, with a reasonable degree of certainty, to the broader population. In contrast, most qualitative studies rely on samples not chosen at random.

The decision to study a specific organization or culture dictates the pool of participants. For example, if you want to study in depth a merger involving two companies, you will interview people from those companies. Likewise, if you decide to investigate the culture of the inhabitants of a particular ethnic neighborhood, your study participants will come from that locale. Finally, if you decide to do action research in an organization, your participants will come primarily from within that organization. As you can see, a nonrandom sample is often the result of a choice to do qualitative research.

Reliability speaks to one's level of confidence that a study, if replicated by another researcher, would yield the same results. A reliable research design, by definition, is replicable. In practice, the issue of reliability, like the issues of internal and external validity, is central to the quality of any proposed research. You must present evidence in your dissertation proposal that the measurement instruments you use in a quantitative study or the interview protocols you use to collect your data in a qualitative study are reliable.

Population and Sample

Two of the main characteristics of an ideal sample are that it is representative and chosen at random from the population. In effect, your sample should statistically resemble (i.e., be representative of) the population. This ensures that you are studying a cross section of the population, not an unrepresentative subset. Also, you should select your sample at random from the set of possible study participants in the population. Randomness is a requirement for the validity of the statistics that you will use to analyze your data. Together, these two sample characteristics provide the foundation for drawing statistically valid inferences from the sample statistics about the population parameters.

Data Collection and Analysis

As mentioned earlier, you must clearly specify in your proposal how you will collect and analyze your data. Furthermore, your approach must follow the guidelines laid out in your methodological guide, such as Babbie (1990) for surveys, Lipsey & Wilson (2001) for meta-analysis, or Yin (2003) for case studies.

Presentation of Findings

Every doctoral program has, or should have, a set of very specific guidelines for presenting the findings of a research project, particularly the dissertation. These relate to the overall structure of the final product, which often follows the format of a journal article, as well specific requirements for content, formatting, and style.

The typical structure for a dissertation consists of five interrelated chapters that deal, respectively, with (a) an introduction or overview of the key elements of the study, (b) a comprehensive literature review, (c) a detailed description of the research method, (d) an explanation of the findings or results of the study, and (e) the conclusions and recommendations for further study that follow from these findings.

Note that the dissertation proposal consists of the first three chapters of the dissertation, which you write prior to conducting the actual research. After your dissertation committee, the Institutional Review Board (IRB), which oversees all research to ensure its acceptability, and any other powers that be at your university involved in the process approve your dissertation, you conduct the research. Then, you write the last two chapters and submit the final product, which consists of all five chapters of your dissertation.

Iterative Nature of the Process

This six-step research process seems deceptively linear. In practice, it is a highly iterative, trial-and-error process of working with all of the elements until they fit into a coherent whole. Expect to examine many potential dissertation ideas using this process before you find one that works. Expect to revise the steps in the process in response to knew insights, suggestions from reviewers, changes in personal circumstances, and the like. Work hard to get them to converge so that you can complete a high quality dissertation and graduate.

For more on the subject of iterative research design, consult the resources section at the end of the book.

The GOAL—Design, Conduct, and Report

As you know by now, the goal of your dissertation research is to demonstrate to your institution that you can design, conduct, and report on the findings of a research project. In so doing, you show your competence in the research process and prove yourself worthy of the title of doctor of philosophy.

Knowing the six steps in the research process (listed below for ease of reference) and the secrets for using them in dissertation research (presented earlier) will enable you to accelerate dramatically your doctoral program.

The steps in the research process are:

1. Problem Statement
2. Literature Search
3. Purpose Statement
4. Research Questions/Hypotheses
5. Research Method
6. Research Design

Note: There is still more that you can do to move things along, as we shall see in the next chapter, which deals with human side of the dissertation process.

Chapter 7

Managing the Dissertation Process

Your committee members are people, not just distinguished academicians. Keeping this in mind will help you to deal with them in a manner that satisfies your objectives and meets their needs. To that end, we will discuss a number of strategies for selecting and working effectively with your dissertation committee in this section. These will include:

- Committee Selection
- Process Management
- Conflict Resolution

Committee Selection

Take every opportunity you can early in your program to meet the faculty in your area of interest, especially if you are pursuing your doctorate via a distance education program, to determine which of them you might want on your dissertation committee. If you think someone is a potential candidate, if possible, ask him or her to assess one of your major papers to determine if you work well together. At a minimum, try to meet as many of the faculty who meet your decision criteria as possible. Some of the decision criteria you might consider in selecting committee members are:

- Expertise
- Chemistry
- Responsiveness

- Interest and Availability

Expertise

You want faculty on your committee who have content and methodological expertise. A content person will help you to (a) ground your research in the literature, (b) design a research project that has the potential to add knew knowledge to the field, and (c) interpret the meaning of your findings. A methodology expert will help you to design a research study to answer your research questions or test your hypotheses that follows accepted research methods and, hence, has internal validity, reliability, and external validity (i.e., generalizability).

Note that you should have both sets of expertise, content and methodology, available to you from members of your committee. But this does not mean that you need a content person and a methodologist on your committee, although this may be necessary. In some cases, one person may provide both types of expertise.

Chemistry

Other than the obvious need to find faculty with the expertise you need to help you complete your dissertation, it is imperative that you relate and work well with each person on your committee. Because completing a dissertation is a time consuming and very demanding activity, think of your committee, especially your chair, as potential colleagues rather than as mere advisors. If you find a highly qualified faculty member who could provide needed expertise, but with whom you don't relate well, run, don't walk away as fast as you can. Life is just too short to take on this aggravation.

Ideally, you will want to construct a harmonious committee. Your dissertation chair can really help you to find the right people with the right chemistry. After all, he or she will be the primary guide on your doctoral journey. To assist your chair in this endeavor, put together a preliminary list of candidates using these or other criteria. However, be flexible and expect your chair to have a major say about which of these faculty members, or others that you may not have considered, he would like to see on your committee.

Expertise and chemistry are characteristics that occur to most students when they are considering potential dissertation committee members. However, many students fail to consider responsiveness.

Responsiveness

One of the essential characteristics of a good committee member is responsiveness. There are many ways to determine if a given faculty member is responsive, including (a) working with the individual, (b) talking with other students who have worked with or had the person as an instructor, (c) sending an email or leaving a voice mail message to test unobtrusively the person's responsiveness, or, if you prefer the direct approach, (d) just asking the faculty member about his or her policy on responding to students.

Take your pick of methods, but don't fail to determine the responsiveness of each potential member of your committee. Otherwise, in the middle of you dissertation process, when your patience is at its ebb from waiting for what seems like an interminable time for a response, you will regret your lack of diligence.

Interest and Availability

Once you have made your selections, you can ask each of the faculty on your list if they would be willing to serve on your committee. Each request should include an overview or prospectus summarizing your proposed dissertation project so that the faculty member can see what you are asking him or her to sign on for.

Be respectful of faculty commitments and don't take offense if some of them are not interested in your study or are not available to serve on your committee. In that case, just move on to others on your list. Continue until you have assembled your team.

Process Management

Who is in charge of your dissertation process, you, your dissertation chair, or the other committee members?

Simply put, you must take charge of the process. After all, you are the one who wants to complete it and earn your Ph.D. Besides completing all of the requirements for the degree, being in charge means submitting all required administrative paperwork that is not the direct responsibility of your chair to submit. However, being in charge does not mean that you control the work of your dissertation committee directly. Your chair will play the role of committee facilitator.

For example, you and the chair will work on your dissertation proposal (and later the full dissertation) together. When the chair says the proposal is ready, he or she will then either send it to the other members of the committee on your behalf or, more typically, direct you to do so. From that point on, you will interact with the committee when and only as agreed upon with your chair until the process is completed.

Having your chair direct the process of interacting with the committee will not preclude your having direct contact with your content and methodology experts whenever necessary. On the contrary, it will ensure a smoother, better controlled process by having a single point of contact, the chair, for you and the members of your committee.

As you can imagine, a great chair skilled at selecting and working with committee members can make a significant difference to you and your progress toward the degree. So, make sure you find the very best one you can.

In my opinion, chemistry and responsiveness are the key criteria for selecting a dissertation chair; far outweighing expertise in importance. You can always stack the committee with content and methodological expertise if your chair is not deep in those areas relevant to your dissertation topic.

Conflict Resolution

Imagine that, despite your best efforts, things get out of control at some point in the dissertation process. Say, for instance, that two members of your committee disagree on what each considers is an important aspect of your dissertation. To satisfy one, you must dissatisfy the other. What do you do?

Whether your process is based on a consensus model or not, I suggest that you immediately involve your dissertation chair in a conflict resolution process designed to get all of the members of your dissertation committee, including the two at odds, to agree on what you need to change and how. If you make unilateral changes in response to either member's request, you will be revising constantly and never completely satisfy your committee.

Remember that consensus does not mean unanimous agreement. Consensus means that everyone either agrees on what you have to do or is neutral but can live with the group's decision. This important outcome is, surprisingly, not as difficult to achieve as some people believe, especially when the members engage in a collaborative process of discussing the problem and determining a solution. A face-to-face meeting of the committee (or a telephone conference call) is a very good method for resolving these knotty problems by consensus because it simultaneously engages all of the committee members in the conflict resolution process.

Chapter 8

More Ways to Accelerate a Program

As you know now, there are many ways to accelerate your transition from a student to a scholar. In the previous sections, we examined a number of them in relation to various aspects of the doctoral journey, such as writing your major papers and your dissertation. In this section, we discuss several other ideas that, if properly implemented, can enhance your performance and accelerate your progress toward the coveted doctoral degree:

- Improve Your Writing
- Learn Basic Statistics
- Familiarize Yourself with Technology
- Sharpen Your Time Management Skills
- Read Other Students' Dissertations
- Attend a Graduation Ceremony
- Behave Ethically

Improve Your Writing

Good doctoral writing is hard to find. Yet, as you know, it is one of the ways that true scholars distinguish themselves from others. Furthermore, good writing that adheres to the formatting and style guidelines of your university will make it easier for your readers to focus on your content (i.e., your ideas). This, in turn, will dramatically reduce revision time and, therefore, time to graduation.

If you are not a good writer, take a writing course before you get too far into your doctoral program or, better still, prior to undertaking it. If you are rusty, reread Stunk and White's *The Elements of Style*. If you know don't know the rules of the style your university requires you to write in (such as APA or Turabian), then learn them. If you are familiar with them but not current, buy the latest manual and brush up.

Finally, make every effort to identify and master the specific formatting requirements of your university, which often supersede aspects of other, more universal styles, like APA. These university-specific guidelines will cover things like acceptable fonts and font-sizes, text spacing, and paragraph indentation.

While these are not major items, getting them wrong can doom you to unnecessary revisions; while getting them right the first time will mark you as a scholar. Like it or not, a scholar has to pay attention to these details and get them right. Someone, in the words of the idiom, has to dot the i's and cross the t's. You, as a Ph.D. student, are that person.

Caveat: Students sometimes employ writing coaches or editors to help them prepare their major papers or dissertation. While this may enable you to complete your dissertation more quickly, and hence be worth the additional expense, it will not make you a better writer. And, as we have seen, being a good writer will greatly enhance your career as a scholar. So, consider the option of hiring someone to revise your work in addition to, rather than in lieu of, taking direct measures to improve your writing.

Learn Basic Statistics

If your doctoral program requires you to take a course in statistics or data analysis, which you will need to interpret the findings of empirical research (yours and others), then it is a very good idea to brush up on your math and statistics *before* you take that course. I teach a required, doctoral-level data analysis/statistics course, and I can say without hesitation that most students find it extremely demanding and very stressful.

Unfortunately, most students who dislike or dread mathematics prefer to minimize their exposure to it. So, they instinctively avoid courses in subjects like statistics. If you are one of these people and you are facing a required, doctoral-level statistics course that you must pass, my advice is to weigh the minor additional cost and stress of taking an optional, introductory statistics course before you start your program or early in it (when you have more time and energy) against the stress and difficulty of taking an advanced course, in a do-or-die mode, in the middle of your program (when your time is arguably more limited and your energy level lower).

Most students do not take this approach and, therefore, pay a heavy price in terms of added stress and extra effort. I have often felt that they would have been better off it they had brushed up on their statistics before attempting their doctoral seminar.

Familiarize Yourself with Technology

The PC and the Internet are undeniably keys to the 21st century. As such, you must attempt to master their use if you want to accelerate your doctoral program. If you are computer phobic, you will never make it. Choose to join the children and the increasing numbers of plugged-in, computer literate adults working on the World Wide Web.

Your goal is to master the incredible variety of time-saving software that exists and is directly applicable to your doctoral program. This begins with understanding and exploiting the features of Microsoft Word, Excel, and PowerPoint; software which provide the means to produce quality documents, spreadsheets, and slide presentations, respectively.

In addition, software written specifically for doctoral students, like EndNote, will enable you to keep track of the references you cite in your documents and, thereby, greatly facilitate the creation of bibliographies and reference lists for your major papers, dissertation, and journal articles.

Note that there is a difference between a bibliography and a reference list. While the citations provided in bibliographies and reference lists are the same, you use the word "Bibliography" as the header for your list of references if your list includes not only the works of authors you cited in your paper, but also other works not mentioned or cited (e.g., in a learning agreement where you are proposing to read certain documents). However, if your reference list contains the complete citations for only the published works of the scholars cited in your work, then it is appropriate to use the word "References" as the header (e.g., in a major paper, dissertation, or journal article).

Sharpen Your Time Management Skills

It seems that everyone has taken a time management course at one point in their careers. If you have, then it is time to brush up on these skills. If not, then do some research, find a course that suits your temperament, study it, and apply its principles to your program. Because balancing the demands of the doctoral journey with all of life's other demands is really one big exercise in time management, time spent mastering and applying these fundamental skills will surely result in your achieving your goal more expeditiously and with less effort.

Read Other Students' Dissertations

One of the best ways to begin your dissertation on day 1 is to acquire and read several dissertations published by graduates of your university. Perhaps some of your faculty members are graduates. Their dissertations should make interesting reading. How about prize-winning dissertations from recent graduates? These will certainly provide insights into what your university considers to be a good dissertation. How about dissertations by graduates who have done work in your area of interest? Surely they will give you a feel for the type of work required in your dissertation research. They will also provide valuable insights into the literature in your field of interest. Finally, each dissertation will illustrate the application of those all important style and formatting guidelines to which you must adhere.

Attend a Graduation Ceremony

If you want a big boost of energy and motivation to persist, attend a graduation ceremony for doctoral students in your university early in your program. There is nothing quite like watching those proud and happy people accept their degrees to motivate you to work hard and smart to become one of them.

The vision of yourself crossing that stage and receiving your doctoral hood will sustain you at times when the struggle seems overwhelming. Early in my program, I took the time from a busy residency schedule to attend a graduation ceremony at the suggestion of a more advanced, and very wise, fellow student. It proved to be a most inspiring event and an excellent use of my time.

Behave Ethically

What can I say? Either you are honest or you are not. As a doctor of philosophy, people will assume that you act responsibly and ethically, and well they should. At the risk of preaching to the choir, I urge you to be honest, fair, responsible, and ethical in your doctoral studies and everything else you do, regardless of the pressure to do otherwise. Your integrity is simply not for sale, nor should it ever be.

Before I descend from my soap box, I want to ask you to consider what ethical behavior means in one, very practical area—plagiarism. I know that you would never intentionally use the work of others in your own work without giving them proper credit. Sometimes, proper credit takes the form of a direct quotation and an in-text citation (in proper APA style, of course), together with a full reference citation in the reference list or bibliography (also in proper APA style). This form of acknowledgement is required when you feel that the author's own words convey exactly what you want to say in a way that you could not paraphrase effectively.

Note, however, that you cannot string together one quote after another in doctoral work. Instead, you must demonstrate your own critical thinking by correctly paraphrasing the work of others and inserting your critical commentary (involving comparison, contrasting, analysis, synthesis, and evaluation) on their work.

Thus, as a scholar you need to learn how to paraphrase the ideas and arguments of others. That is, to convey the essence of other people's ideas in your own words. Unfortunately, if you do not do this properly, you can inadvertently be guilty of plagiarism. Let us spend a few minutes examining the two major ways in which this can occur.

First, when you paraphrase, you must provide a correct in-text and reference citation, just like you do when you quote somebody. Not realizing this, some students fail to provide the necessary citations; thus creating in the minds of their readers the impression that the ideas are in fact their own, rather than someone else's.

As you may recall, the doctoral reader will assume by convention that every single thing word that you do not attribute directly by citation to somebody else is your idea. If it is not your idea, then you have plagiarized. So, be safe, provide appropriate citations for all ideas that are not yours in all of your doctoral work (e.g., papers, online class discussion postings, dissertations).

However, providing in-text and reference citations for your paraphrases is not enough. In addition, you must choose the words in a paraphrase carefully, or once again be inadvertently guilty of plagiarism. A correct paraphrase is primarily in your own words. One that isn't is primarily in the words of the original author. So, do not fall into the habit of inserting others work into your documents and changing one or two words. If you do, whether or not you provide the proper citations, you will be guilty of plagiarism.

One trick to help you avoid incorrect paraphrasing that helps many students is to read the selection, then physically put the book, article, or dissertation aside *before* (a) writing down the gist of it in your own words and (b) adding the required in-text and bibliographic reference citations.

When you apply these suggestions for avoiding plagiarism, your text will consist of (a) a small percentage of direct quotations from the work of others (appropriately cited), (b) properly paraphrased (i.e., in your own words) material from the work of others (appropriately cited), and (c) your own, original ideas (without citation, of course).

If you do this properly, the doctoral reader will be able to distinguish clearly between your thoughts, the work of other scholars you have paraphrased and presented to support your ideas and arguments, and the exact words of other scholars you have used to develop and support your arguments.

To reiterate, you are responsible as a scholar to apply the highest possible ethical standards to everything you do. I urge you never to settle for less for any reason at any time during your doctoral journey.

What's Next?

While I cannot guarantee that they will help you to complete your degree in record time, I sincerely believe that the ideas I have shared with you in this book can enable you to work at higher level, learn more, and obtain your doctoral degree more quickly and easily than would otherwise have been possible.

If these ideas work well for you and you want to share what you have learned with other doctoral students, I hope you will take the time contribute to the blog at my web site (www.mindfirepress.com). Also, if you have suggestions for enhancing later editions of this book, please email them to DrL@mindfirepress.com.

Finally, I hope that as a true scholar you will use the knowledge you acquire in your doctoral journey to make the world a better place.

References

Babbie, E. (1990). *Survey research methods* (2nd ed.).
Belmont, CA: Wadsworth Publishing Company.

Boyer, E. L. (1990). *Scholarship reconsidered: Priorities
of the professoriate.* San Francisco, CA: Jossey-Bass
Publishers.

Burke, W. W. (1982). *Organization development: Principles and practices.* Boston: Little, Brown and Company.

Levasseur, R. E. (2004). *The impact of a transforming
leadership style on follower performance and satisfaction: A meta-analysis.* Ann Arbor: UMI Dissertation Services.

Lipsey, M. W., & Wilson, D. B. (2001). *Practical meta-
analysis.* Thousand Oaks: Sage.

Maslow, A. (1954). *Motivation and personality.* New
York: Harper and Row.

Strunk, W., & White, E. B. (1979). *The elements of style.*
New York: Macmillan Publishing Company, Inc.

Yin, R. K. (2003). *Case study research: Design and
methods* (3rd ed.). Thousand Oaks: Sage.

Resources

Sadly, there are few good resources available for doctoral students. However, here are a few that you may find helpful.

APA

Robert Perrin has a book that I use at least 90% of the time when I need to look up how to format something properly in APA style. It is entitled *Pocket Guide to APA Style*. Among its many features are (a) a spiral binding (which means you can lay it down on a flat surface and it will remain open to the page you are referencing), (b) a convenient size, (c) a reasonable price, (d) and a convenient structure which organizes citation information into separate areas for periodicals, books, and electronic sources, respectively.

Basic Statistics

As a statistics instructor at the undergraduate and graduate level, I have scoured the bookshelves for useful introductory texts on the subject. Unfortunately, the many so-called elementary texts don't really make the subject less threatening or obscure. Therefore, I have written a book to fill the void.

Entitled *Practical Statistics*, this book is for beginners. It provides them with a basic understanding of the subject (a) so that they can better interpret the statistics the find in the newspapers, books, and magazines they read every day and (b) so that they can better prepare themselves for the rigors of advanced statistical studies, if necessary. You can read more about this book at my web site, www.mindfirepress.com.

Effecting Positive Social Change

Many people want to make a difference in the world. If you do too, then, as a doctoral student, you may find my new, research-based book on the subject particularly interesting. First, it is an attempt to integrate scholarly theories and research on transforming leadership into a set of guiding principles for leadership and change in the new millennium. Second, the first part of the book is in proper APA style. Hence, like the example in the appendix, it illustrates doctoral–level thinking and writing.

The book is entitled *Leadership and Change in the 21st Century*. For more information about it, visit my web site, www.mindfirepress.com.

EndNote for Students

As I mentioned earlier, I found this software to be extremely helpful in capturing all of the references of value I discovered in my doctoral work in APA style in one place. I am not saying this is the only or the best software, just that I found it easy to work with, at least for the simple uses I have put it to. EndNote has additional functionality that I have not used that you may or may not find useful. But, whether you use EndNote, some similar software, or a general program like Microsoft Word, I do recommend that you keep track of your bibliographic references, in correct alphabetical order, for your use in writing major papers, articles, or your dissertation.

Iterative Research Design

The best book on research design I have read is Joseph Maxwell's *Qualitative Research Design: An Iterative Approach*. Don't let the title fool you. The real focus of this book is iterative research design, not qualitative methods. It is the only book I have found that presents the design process as an iterative, rather than a linear, approach. Besides explaining how to fit all of the pieces of the dissertation puzzle together in an iterative fashion, Maxwell provides a very useful diagramming technique that will help you to keep those pieces and their interconnections clearly in focus throughout the research design process.

For more on Maxwell's approach, read the sample paper in the appendix, which contains an application of its principles to the development of a case study on leadership and organizational change.

Appendix

A Section of a Major Paper

This appendix contains the theoretical foundation section of a paper on leadership and organizational change written in correct APA style and in accordance with the formatting requirements of a major online university.

An example of scholarly writing, I have provided this paper to help you understand how to apply the ideas presented in the book. If you decide to incorporate information contained in this essay in your own work, remember to provide proper in-text and reference citations, whether you quote directly or paraphrase.

Theoretical Foundation for a Case Study

Table of Contents

Introduction

This research paper is about transformational leadership. Specifically, it is about how the leaders of three diverse organizations, responded to organizational conditions that demanded dramatic and visionary action to ensure their long-run survival and success. To help assess the quality of the actions taken by the leaders of these organizations in their moments of crisis, the first part of this paper will focus on (a) the principles of modern leadership, management, and organizational change, (b) the role of culture in organizational management, and (c) the impact of the environment on organizational decision making.

The second part will explore the history and management processes of each organization to provide a context for analyzing the actions taken by their respective leaders at crucial times in the history of each organization. A comparison of each of the three cases in point will yield insights into (a) the nature of organizational leadership in practice, (b) the implications for leadership theory and research, and (c) the value of case study research. These lessons learned will provide input into future research into the leadership and management of public, private, and non-governmental organizations.

Case Study Research

This section examines the elements of case study research that shaped the research reported in this paper. The fundamental approach to qualitative research proposed by Maxwell (1996) forms the basis for this case study. Specifically, Maxwell (1996, pp. 4–8) presents a model of qualitative research design which has five, interrelated parts: (a) purposes of the research, (b) conceptual or theoretical context for the research, (c) research questions, (d) research methods, and (e) efforts to ensure the validity of the research.

The table below lists the key question that Maxwell (1996) asks in each phase of the research. Note that each is the heading of a chapter in the book.

Step	Label	Key Question
1	Purposes	Why are you doing this study?
2	Conceptual Context	What do you think is going on?
3	Research Questions	What do you want to understand?
4	Methods	What will you actually do?
5	Validity	How might you be wrong?

It is important to note that this model identifies the steps in an interactive and iterative approach to design (Maxwell, 1996, p. 8). That is, the parts of the model are interrelated and, therefore, a change in one may necessitate a change in one or more of the other parts. Also, as the research progresses, it may require a change in a preceding step. For example, during the application or methods stage, a discovery of unexpected and important data may reshape the purposes or research questions. This flexibility to change the design is an important aspect of qualitative research.

Yin (2003) provides the rationale for using a case study approach to examine the why and how of what happened at key moments in the history of these three organizations. Specifically, Yin (2003) argued that "in general, case studies are the preferred strategy when 'how' and 'why' questions are being posed, when the investigator has little control over events, and when the focus is on a contemporary phenomenon within some real-life context" (p. 1).

In this research, questions about what happened and why are the principal foci of the investigation. Furthermore, the researcher has no control of the events that took place in these three organizations. Finally, the issue of how leaders of in three distinctly different major organizations confront the need to transform them to meet the changing demands of a competitive environment certainly qualifies as an important contemporary phenomenon worthy of study.

Yin (2003) also provides an important methodological input to this study with regard to the importance of using multiple sources of evidence to triangulate or confirm the validity of the data and the conclusions based on them. In particular, Yin (2003, p. 85–96) identified six major sources of evidence: (a) documentation, such as letters, reports, or studies; (b) archival records, such as budgets, financial statements, and personnel records; (c) open-ended interviews with informants; (d) direct observations or field visits to the "case study site;" (e) more active, participant observation, such as functioning as a staff member (or consulting to the leader of the organization in this particular study); and (f) physical evidence or cultural artifacts, such as one might collect in an archeological expedition.

An organizational example of the latter might be the dress code observed by the managers in the organization. The use of as many of these sources of evidence in the case study research as possible is an acknowledgement of their importance to the validity of the data and findings.

Having used Yin (2003) to establish the rationale for doing a case study and to emphasize the importance of collecting evidence from multiple sources (i.e., triangulating), the next step is to answer the five questions raised by Maxwell (1996) with regard to this particular research design. First, the primary purposes for doing this study are to compare the management practices in three organizations in widely separated arenas (i.e., the private sector, the public sector, and the non-governmental sector) and to examine the applicability of modern leadership and organizational change theories to the transformation of major organizations by exploring what happened (or did not) in each organization and why in relation to the standards implicit in these theories.

Maxwell (1996, p. 4) indicates that the second component of the research design (which deals with the theoretical foundation for the study) should be based on the experience of the researcher, existing theory and research, results of pilot studies or other investigations, and thought experiments. In this instance, theories about effective leadership, management, and organizational change, theories about the role of culture in organization management, and the systemic theory of strategic contingency, which deals with the need to fit strategy to the demands of the environment, provide the principal theoretical context for the study.

The third element of the research design involves the research questions. For this investigation, the primary research questions are:

1. What factors in each organization or its environment led to the major crisis faced by the organization?

2. What are the similarities and differences in how the leaders in each organization dealt with the need to transform their organization at a crucial point in its history?

3. What actions were taken in each case and why were they successful or unsuccessful?

4. How do these management actions and their outcomes compare to the actions and results suggested by the foremost theories of leadership and organizational change?

5. What lessons can be learned from this study about the practice of management in times that call for major organizational change, about the real-world applicability of leadership theories, and about the utility of the case study method for researching problems of this kind.

The fourth component of the research design consists of the methods of data collection. In this study, this involved a combination of the five of the six sources of evidence described by Yin (2003) as indicated in the following table.

Organization	A	B	C
Documents	Yes	Yes	Yes
Records	No	Yes	Yes
Interviews	Yes	Yes	No
Observations	No	Yes	Yes
Participation	No	Yes	Yes

The sixth element of the approach to research design recommended by Maxwell (1996) involves attention to validity. Triangulation of sources (at least two in each mini-case), sites (three separate organizations in separate areas of the business world), and theories (leadership, organizational change, cultural impact, and strategic contingency) adds to the intrinsic validity of the study. Furthermore, a search for contradictory explanations for the phenomena observed in each case enhances the intrinsic validity of the study.

Modern Leadership Theory

To analyze what happened at the three organizations and make sense of the findings, it is necessary to have a theoretical foundation in modern leadership theory. Old fashioned ideas about born leaders, like Abraham Lincoln, Martin Luther King, Gandhi, and John F. Kennedy, arising magically to save the day are passé. New theories, more suited to the rapid pace of change in the 21st century, have replaced them.

Despite the growing need for leaders who can bring about effective organizational and social change to meet the demands of a rapidly changing environment, there appears to be a scarcity of leaders up to challenges of managing in this new era.

> Thanks to globalization we can now talk about the end of leadership as we know it without the risk of hyperbole . . . top-down leadership is not only wrong, unrealistic, and maladaptive, but also dangerous. This form of leadership will erode competi-

tive advantage and destroy the aspirations of any leader or organization. (Bennis, 1999, p. 7)

There is a clear need to identify ways to enhance the capabilities of contemporary leaders to deal with the new challenges they face. The question is how to do it.

Bennis (1999) has an answer: "This top-down tendency is dysfunctional in today's world of blurring change, and will get us into unspeakable trouble unless we understand that the search engine for effective change is the workforce and their creative alliance with top leadership" (pp. 8–9). In the past, many leaders managed change effectively in one of two basic ways: (a) by using a form of inspirational, top-down leadership known as transformational leadership (Bass, 1990) or (b) by employing a bottom-up approach that uses well-defined, participative processes to engage participants actively in the change effort (Burke, 1987).

However, few leaders blended both approaches into the same intervention, despite the fact that research findings strongly support the benefits of each approach (e.g., Dvir, Avolio, and Shamir (2002) provided support for the efficacy of transformational leadership while Johnson and Johnson (1989) presented considerable evidence of the benefits of cooperative approaches in terms of higher performance and greater member satisfaction) and that the practice of change management supports the synergies that result when they are combined in the same change effort (Bradford & Cohen, 1984).

To provide an impetus for leaders of the future to capitalize on the synergies possible from a creative synthesis of these two powerful approaches to change, there is a clear need to study the joint impact of transformational leadership style and participative change management process on organizational performance and member satisfaction.

The standard developed in this part of the Case Study is an attempt to integrate these two bodies of knowledge into a coherent whole which can serve (a) as a standard or yardstick for measuring the actions of the leaders in each of the cases in point in part two of this paper as well as (b) the foundation for an integrated theory of leadership style and participative change management that can be assessed by future research.

Transformational Leadership

A topic of interest to many researchers over the years has been how to improve the effectiveness of organizational leaders. In 1978, James MacGregor Burns won a

Pulitzer Prize for a book (Burns, 1978) about a new form of leadership, called transforming leadership, which engages the follower as a whole person in the process of achieving organizational and societal goals. The goal of the transforming leader is no less than to "produce social change that will satisfy followers' authentic needs" (Burns, 1978, p. 3).

Recognizing the intrinsic power of this concept, researchers enhanced the theory and conducted studies to measure the effects of transformational leadership (Avolio, Waldman, & Yammarino, 1991; Bass, 1990; Dvir, Avolio, & Shamir, 2002). Bass (1990) reported on a study of the willingness of employees in a large engineering firm to make extra efforts on the job as a function of the leadership style of their managers. Bass found that employees who rated their managers as highly transformational were more likely to make the extra effort than employees who worked for non-transformational leaders. As a result, this study provided important empirical evidence of the effectiveness of transformational leadership.

In Avolio, Waldman, and Yammarino (1991, p. 9), the authors enhanced the original conception of transformation leadership to include four explicit dimensions, (a) individual consideration, (b) intellectual stimulation, (c) inspirational motivation, and (d) idealized influence. These dimensions are criteria against which to measure the visions and actions of transformational leaders.

Stronger proof of transformational leadership's effectiveness comes from researchers who recently conducted a longitudinal, randomized, field experiment involving basic military training procedures (Dvir, Avolio, & Shamir, 2002). Dvir et al. wanted to provide additional (more causal) support for the theory of transformational leadership.

> Transformational leadership has been shown to have a positive relationship with performance...Yet a causal relationship between transformational leadership and follower performance has only rarely been demonstrated because prior studies have had static, correlational, or nonexperimental designs. (p. 735)

The authors found that the platoons led by officer cadets trained in transformational leadership performed better and were more highly developed on average than those led by the control group leaders.

These studies show that transformational leadership has a positive impact on the performance, development, and satisfaction of followers. Other studies, conducted to demonstrate the effectiveness of visionary and charismatic leadership, provide additional evidence of the efficacy of transformational leadership if we accept the argument of Dvir, Avolio, and Shamir (2002) that these three forms of leadership constitute a "new genre of leadership theories."

Other Forms of New Genre Leadership

Recently, leadership scholars have acknowledged the close connection between visionary, charismatic, and transformational leadership theories.

> It can be safely concluded that there is a strong convergence of the findings from studies with charismatic leadership and those concerned with transformational and visionary leadership." (House & Shamir, 1993, p. 84)

Carl and Javidian (2001) argued for the universality of charismatic leadership across national boundaries (e.g., Canada, Hungary, Austria, and Sweden). Using data from "2300 managers in eight diverse cultures," the authors performed factor analyses to test a model of charismatic leadership against criteria for universality and found that "a relatively culture-free charismatic leader profile does exist" and that "it is comprised of the constructs of a vision, motivation, and proactivity." (Carl & Javidian, 2001, p. B1).

According to the authors, the visionary factor "consisted of visionary, willful, and performance oriented," the motivation factor "consisted of confidence builder, enthusiastic, motive arouser, and intellectually stimulating," and the proactivity factor consisted of "foresight, plans ahead, logical, and intuitive" (Carl and Javidian, 2001, p. B5). To summarize, vision, motivation, and proactivity—which are associated with charismatic leadership in a wide range of cultures—are the principal characteristics of the new genre of leadership according to Carl and Javidian (2001).

Based on the findings of Carl and Javidian (2001), new genre leadership might be expected to work in public sector organizations even though they represent a different "culture" than the private sector, military, or educational organizations on which Bass (1990) and other advocates of transformational leadership, such as Dvir, Avolio, and Shamir (2002), tested the theory.

However, Javidian and Waldman (2003) studied charismatic leadership in fifty Canadian public sector organizations and found that "while charismatic leadership is more or less similarly conceived in the public sector, it may not necessarily produce the types of per-

formance or motivational results that are typically associated with it in private sector organizations" (p. 239).

They attribute this difference in outcomes to the
fact that in public sector organizations "charismatic
leaders may be constrained in their behavior or accom-
plishments because of political or bureaucratic considerations" (Javidian & Waldman, 2003, p. 239). The authors
speculate that the lack of urgency or crisis in most public
sector organizations mitigates the effects of charismatic
leadership.

Following this logic, in times of crisis the outcomes
in the public sector are more likely to be representative of
outcomes achieved by leaders in the private sector.

To provide a causal connection between charismatic
leadership and its impact on followers, Pillai and Meindl
(1991) examined in a laboratory experiment the effect of a
crisis on charismatic leadership. They discovered that
"subjects that experienced a crisis during a group task
selected leaders more on the basis of their charismatic
appeal than those who did not experience a crisis. In turn,
leaders perceived to be more charismatic received higher
ratings of effectiveness and satisfaction" (Pillai & Meindl,
1991, p. 235).

So it might be argued with some confidence that crisis, an increasingly common aspect of the environment for organizations in the 21st century (whether in the public or private sector), supports the emergence and ultimate success of transformational leaders.

Two areas that charismatic, visionary, or transformational (i.e., new genre) leadership, whether induced by a crisis or not, should affect positively are the people and the productivity of the organization. Parry (2000, p. 39) analyzed the results of the 1999 New Zealand Leadership Survey and discovered a high correlation between transformational leadership and follower motivation (0.76), the followers belief in the ability of the leader (0.56), and the presence of a strong, positive organizational culture (0.52).

On the productivity side, Parry (2000) found a moderate correlation between leadership quality and the perception by followers that the organization achieved its bottom line (0.34). The author explained the significance of this finding as follows:

> Leadership has a smaller impact on perceptions that the organization achieves its bottom-line . . . This is because the bottom-line is affected by things other than leadership . . . However, the relationship

between (transformational) leadership and the bottom-line is still quite considerable. (Parry, 2000, p. 39)

Jung and Avolio (2000) performed an experiment to test the causal link between transformational leadership and performance. There findings were similar to those of Pillai and Meindl (1991). Based on path analyses, Jung and Avolio (2000) found that "transformational leadership had both direct and indirect effects on performance mediated through followers trust in the leaders and value congruence" (p. 949). Thus, the study confirmed the link between transformational leadership (versus transactional leadership) and performance.

Interestingly, the effect of the hypothesized mediator variables of trust and value congruence was not significant in this study. However, as the authors point out, this is probably due to the short duration of the activity (a single class activity) and the fact that the participants had no history with the leaders and, therefore, had very little time to establish trust or determine value congruence.

Based on the evidence provided in the research studies described in this section, it is fair to say that new genre leadership (i.e., charismatic, visionary, and trans-

formational leadership) works in many types of organizations in many cultures to improve performance and member satisfaction.

In the next section, the important role of change
management theory and cooperative or participative
processes in facilitating organizational transformation
and, thereby, enhancing the impact of transformational
leadership becomes the focus of attention.

Organizational Change Theory

According to Schein (1999), Kurt Lewin once said,
"There is nothing so practical as a good theory." Schein, a
professor at the MIT Sloan School greatly admires Lewin.

> The power of Lewin's theorizing lay not in a formal
> propositional kind of theory but in his ability to
> "build" models of processes that drew attention to
> the right kind of variables that needed to be con-
> ceptualized and observed. In my opinion, the most
> powerful of these (theories) was his model of the
> change process in human systems. (Schein, 1999, p.
> 59)

A classic model of change, the three-stage model of
Kurt Lewin (Burke, 1987, pp. 54–56), hypothesizes that
change happens in three steps or stages. The first step
requires an unfreezing of the current state. Unfreezing
the status quo permits movement or change to occur in

the second step. Finally, the refreezing of new behaviors is the final step. This prevents a reversion to old ways and habits.

Although Lewin postulated the model over fifty years ago, the Lewin model is nonetheless the basis for many current models of leadership and change. For example, John Kotter, a professor at Harvard Business School, in a recent book (Kotter, 1996), developed an eight-stage model that follows the "unfreezing, movement, refreezing" sequence of the Lewin model.

Kotter (1996) described a leadership theory and strategic change process that integrates many of the key elements of a modern leadership and change manage-ment. According to Kotter (1996, p, 21), the eight steps are:

1. Establish a sense of urgency.
2. Create a guiding coalition.
3. Develop a vision and strategy.
4. Communicate the change vision.
5. Empower broad-based action.
6. Generate short-term wins.
7. Consolidate gains and produce more change.
8. Anchor new approaches in the culture.

Clearly, the Kotter (1996) model embeds the three-stage change model of Kurt Lewin—unfreezing, movement, refreezing—described in Burke (1987). Specifically, steps one to four unfreeze, steps five to seven precipitate movement or change, and step eight refreezes.

Thus, the Lewin three-stage model is an important construct for modern, transformational leaders. It provides the critical insight into how change comes about (i.e., through some form of unfreezing event). To Kotter, who deals in the world of CEOs and large corporations, the need to overcome resistance to change suggests the necessity of creating a sense of urgency. But Lewin argued for a different approach when he put forth his theory of change.

Burke (1982) describes the force field analysis method developed by Lewin to capture the personal and environmental forces that affect the behavior of an individual or group. Lewin divided these forces into two opposing categories, driving forces and restraining forces. The driving or helping forces act to motivate a person (or by extension, a group of people) to change; whereas the restraining or hindering forces serve as barriers to change.

Change can occur by adding to or increasing the intensity of the forces Lewin labeled driving forces—that is, forces that push in the desired direction of change—or by diminishing the opposing or restraining forces. Lewin's theory predicts that the better of these two choices is to reduce the intensity of the restraining forces. By adding forces or increasing the intensity of the driving side, a simultaneous increase would occur on the restraining side, and the overall tension level for the system—whether it is a person, a group, or an organization—would intensify. The better choice is then to reduce the restraining forces. (Burke, 1982, p. 31)

Therefore, in Lewinian terms, the Kotter model is flawed by its insistence in step one that a leader create a sense of urgency (which increases the intensity of the driving side, thus leading to increased resistance, a higher level of tension in the system, rather than movement toward the goal).

If not by creating a sense of urgency or otherwise increasing the intensity of the driving forces, how should a leader unfreeze a situation in the first step of a process to bring about meaningful and lasting change? One way to reduce the restraining forces and, thereby, induce movement or change is to use participative processes. Participative processes actively engage participants in the change process in a manner described in the next section.

Group Management and Participative Processes

Many studies have examined the impact of processes that induce cooperation in groups in comparison to processes that instigate competition or create conflict. The results of a meta-analysis of hundreds of such studies (Johnson & Johnson, 1989) provides corroboration for the contention that cooperative processes are far superior to conflict inducing, competitive processes in terms of the performance of group members and their satisfaction with the process.

A central question addressed by this meta-analysis was whether competition (which induces emotional conflict intentionally) improves the outcomes of group activity (i.e., group performance and member satisfaction) more or less than cooperation (which seeks to manage conflict in a supportive way). Johnson and Johnson (1989) found nearly indisputable answers to this question as a result of performing a meta-analytic review of the literature to that date (some 529 research studies). Johnson and Johnson (1989) described their research findings as follows:

On the basis of the research to date (which is considerable), it may be concluded that generally
achievement and productivity were higher in cooperative situations than in competitive or individualistic ones, and that cooperative efforts resulted in
more frequent use of higher-level reasoning strategies, more frequent generation of new ideas and so-
lutions (i.e., process gains), and greater transfer of
learning (i.e., greater productivity on subsequent
similar tasks done individually) than did competitive and individualistic efforts. (p. 171)

Thus, there is much evidence from the literature of
groups to support the effectiveness of using processes that
induce cooperation among the participants in a change
effort.

More support for the power of participative processes to enable meaningful change by facilitating unfreezing, movement, and refreezing comes from the biographer
of Lewin, Alfred J. Morrow, who described an experiment
performed by associates of Lewin at the Harwood Manu-
facturing Company in the late 1940s in Morrow (1969). In
this study, the management (directed by the researchers)
made substantive changes to the jobs of three groups of
workers. These changes affected piece rates and methods
of work, among other factors. One group did not participate, but was simply told of the changes. A second group
was involved in the change process through appointed

representatives. The third group consisted of all of the members of the affected work unit.

> The differences in outcomes of the three (approaches) were clear and dramatic...The consequences in the total-participation group were in sharp contrast to those in the (other) non-participating groups. It regained the pre-change output after only two days and then climbed steadily until it reached a level of about 14% above the earlier average. No one quit; all members of the group worked well with their supervisors, and there were no signs of aggression. (Morrow, 1969, p. 151)

While hardly conclusive in and of itself, this finding nonetheless suggests why organizational development consultants and other change agents who support leaders in their attempts to effect meaningful change in organizations use participative processes.

In summary, the literature on transformational leadership suggests that meaningful change (i.e., transformation) is possible if leaders attend to four aspects of their followers needs in their visions and actions: (a) individual consideration, (b) intellectual stimulation, (c) inspirational motivation, and (d) idealized influence. The literature on change management suggests that meaningful change is possible if leaders unfreeze the situation by reducing the restraining forces preventing necessary change from happening. Finally, the literature on cooperation and the practice of change management suggest that participative processes are a powerful way of reducing these restraining forces.

A creative synthesis of these ideas suggests that combining the power of a transforming vision of the future to unfreeze a situation and initiate change with the power of participative processes to do the same thing might produce a resultant change in performance and satisfaction that exceeds either of the individual approaches, and might even be synergistic. The next section provides some evidence in support of this conclusion.

Integrating Transformational Leadership and Participative Processes

Eisenbach, Watson, and Pillai (1999) argued for the need to link transformational leadership with organizational change methods:

> While change management depends on leadership to be enacted, to date there has been little integration of these two bodies of literature. The key role that leaders play in the change process has been noted by change theorists, yet there is no conclusive research that focuses on the relationship between

leadership and change. (Eisenbach, Watson, & Pillai, 1999, p. 80)

Based on a review of the literatures of leadership and organizational change, the authors concluded that transformational, charismatic, and visionary leadership theories share a common perspective. Namely, that "by articulating a vision, fostering the acceptance of group goals, and providing individualized support, effective leaders change the basic values, beliefs, and attitudes of performers" (Eisenbach, Watson, & Pillai, 1999, p. 83).

This synthesis of the common elements of the "new genre of leadership theories" bears a striking resemblance to the three-step model articulated by Bradford and Cohen (1984). To build strong organizations and effect meaningful change, a leader attempts to do three things (Bradford & Cohen, 1984, pp. 70–98):

1. Build a shared-responsibility team.
2. Develop individual skills continuously.
3. Determine an overarching goal.

By articulating a vision, the leader creates an overarching goal. By fostering the acceptance of group goals, the leader builds a shared-responsibility team. And, by continuously developing the skills of individuals in the group, the leader provides individualized support. In short, Eisenbach, Watson, and Pillai (1999) provide strong evidence of the viability of the Bradford and Cohen leadership and organizational change model, and, therefore, for any integrated leadership theory and strategic change model which incorporates it.

The Role of Culture

Whereas Bradford and Cohen (1984) posit a powerful, intuitive theory of leadership that has a distinctly modern, transformational flavor, Schein (1992), one of the foremost behavioral psychologists and organizational consultants in the world, adds yet another critical variable to the leadership mix. Schein has a simple message for all who would lead effective change: Ignore culture at your peril!

The object of every would-be leader according to Schein (1992) is culture, which is:

> A pattern of shared basic assumptions that the group learned as it solved its problems of external adaptation and internal integration that has worked well enough to be considered valid and, therefore, to be taught to new members as the correct way to perceive, think, and feel in relation to those problems. (p. 12)

Schein has had a long-standing interest in the role of leaders in creating, developing, or changing culture. He maintains that culture and leadership are closely related, and that, in fact, the primary role of the leader is to "create and manage" culture (Schein, 1992, p. 5).

Schein (1992) grounds leadership theory in organizational psychology and organization development to build a unique model that blends the three-stage change model of Kurt Lewin involving unfreezing, movement, and refreezing (Burke, 1987, pp. 54–56) and the notion of organizational growth based on an S-curve (i.e., founding and early growth, midlife, maturity and decline) into the life cycle cultural change strategy for leaders shown in the following table.

Organizational Stage	Change Mechanism
Founding and early growth	1. Incremental change through general and specific evolution
	2. Change through insight from organizational therapy
	3. Change through promotion of hybrids within the culture
Midlife	4. Change through systematic promotion from selected subcultures

	5. Planned change through organization development projects and the creation of organizational learning structures
	6. Unfreezing and change through technological seduction
Maturity and decline	7. Change through infusion of outsiders
	8. Unfreezing through scandal and myth explosion
	9. Change through turn-arounds
	10. Change through coercive persuasion
	11 Destruction and rebirth

(Schein, 1992, p. 304)

The change strategies captured in this table reflect the belief that young organizations, because of the presence of the founders and the likely strength of the culture, can only change effectively from within. Schein (1992), therefore, recommends evolution, self-reflection, and promotion from within as the primary strategies in the early stages of organizational growth. Similarly, the observation that mature organizations become more differentiated into subcultures and, therefore, more likely to be receptive to other change options prompts Schein (1992) to recommend change through planned interventions and seductive educational technologies, like the organizational learning approach of Senge (1990).

Finally, the sense that time is running out on the organization in the maturity and decline phases underlies a series of increasingly radical (to the existing culture) interventions, such as exploding myths about the organization and its leaders or bringing in outsiders to turn things around.

The idea that organizational leadership is most effective if geared to the stage of the organization in its life cycle is a powerful systemic concept that suggests some of the limitations on effective leadership in the real-world. Lawrence and Lorsch (1986) postulated another important situational theory that prescribes leadership behavior in relation to the external environment of the organization—strategic contingency theory.

Strategic Contingency Theory

Lawrence and Lorsch (1986) observed that every organization places different demands on its leaders, all of whom want to ensure the survival and maximum success of their organization, because each faces unique set of demands from its environment. They coined the term "contingency theory" to capture the essential nature of this concept. Based on a careful examination of three effective organizations, the authors concluded that their findings "strongly support" a "contingency theory of organization which recognizes their systemic nature. The basic assumption underlying such a theory... is that organizational variables are in a complex interrelationship with one another and with conditions in the environment" (Lawrence & Lorsch, 1986, p. 157).

Specifically, Lawrence and Lorsch (1986) found that organizational performance depended on the degree to which organizations fit their structure (and internal conflict resolution processes) to the demands of their environment. According to the authors, this "focus...on the fit between organization and its environment...signaled a major shift in the paradigm in organizational behavior (from) 'what is the single best way to manage and organize?'...to 'what is management style and organization form is best suited to a particular situation?'" (Lawrence & Lorsch, 1986, p. ix)

Thus, strategic contingency theory is a broad, general theory that prescribes an approach to leadership and organizational design (i.e., design the organization to fit the environment) without specifying exactly how to do it. Over the years, various researchers in the field have attempted to validate and extend the theory by applying it to specific situations.

The research by Lee and Miller (1996) is noteworthy among the studies performed for this purpose. Lee and Miller (1996) compared the structure and performance of a sample of firms supported by the Korean government to a sample of Korean firms that relied on the application of emergent technologies to survive in highly competitive markets. The authors found that the former tended to choose cost leadership strategies and rely upon established technologies (a strategy which is consistent with a more stable, regulated environment), while the latter tried to fit their strategies to the uncertainties of their market place by focusing on product innovation and superior marketing strategies. Lee and Miller (1996) concluded that "the match between strategy and environment was related to performance, especially in challenging settings" (p. 731). This finding lends credence to the assertion that transformational leadership in response to a critical need will lead to higher performance than transactional leadership in the same situation.

Miller and Cardinal (1994) studied the link between strategic planning and performance. They found "strategic planning to positively affect firm performance" and that "methodological differences across studies have been largely responsible for the inconsistent findings reported in the literature and largely responsible for the debate concerning the value of strategic planning" (p. 1662). Since strategic planning is a formal method used by organizations to match their structure to the demands of their environment, this study lends support to strategic contingency theory.

Amburgey and Dacin (1994) provided confirmation of yet another important aspect of strategic contingency theory; namely, that strategy affects structure and vice versa. In this study, the authors focused on the magnitude and timing of strategic change (as measured by level of diversification) and the magnitude and timing of structural change (as measured by level of decentralization).

According to the Amburgey and Dacin (1994), their study provides "substantial support for the common conception of a contingency relationship between strategy and structure" (p. 1446). Specifically, the authors found that diversification (a strategic change) leads quickly to decentralization (a structural change), and that the reverse is true, but that it takes longer. They also found that "strategy is a much more important determinant of structure than structure is of strategy" (p. 1446). Thus, the findings of this study support strategic contingency theory and the management rubric that "structure follows strategy."

The studies of Amburgey and Dacin (1994), Lee and Miller (1996), and Miller and Cardinal (1994) have provided important evidence in support of the strategic contingency theory of Lawrence and Lorsch (1986). Additional support for the importance and validity of strategic contingency theory to modern leaders comes from Scott (1998):

> Over time, contingency theory has become greatly elaborated . . . as analysts discover more and more factors on which the design of organizations is, or should be, contingent . . . (These factors include) size or scale, technology, geography, uncertainty, individual predispositions of participants, resource dependence, national or cultural differences, scope, and organizational life cycle...(As a result) contingency theory remains the dominant approach to organization design as well as the most widely

utilized contemporary approach to the study of organizations. (p. 97)

In order to transform an organization, the literature reviewed in this component so far suggests that a
leader must simultaneously consider the requirements of
the "new genre" of leadership (i.e., visionary, charismatic,
transformational leadership), Lewinian notions of organizational change, the dictates of organizational culture,
and the demands of the environment. The last section of
this theoretical foundation paper presents an attempt to
integrate these diverse elements of modern leadership
into a coherent whole.

An Integrated Leadership Model

To integrate the major dimensions of leadership
presented in this paper, a simple, step-by-step process is
called for. The following integrated leadership model is a
prescription for the would-be transformational leader in
the 21st century:

1. Scan the environment continuously for major
    threats and opportunities that require immediate
    action to ensure organizational survival and suc-
    cess.

2. Create a powerful, compelling vision of the future that encompasses the ideal organizational response to these key threats and opportunities.

3. Engage the members of the organization in an ongoing dialogue about the vision to keep it current and give them the opportunity to internalize and align with it.

4. Challenge the members of the organization to work together in a collaborative fashion to develop bold action plans to meet these challenges in ways that fit the culture and are consistent with the stage of the organization in its life cycle.

5. Insist that managers and employees share responsibility for the goals, plans, actions, and rewards of the initiatives they take to achieve the vision.

6. Work ceaselessly to develop the capabilities of the individuals, groups, and major components of the organization, as well as the organization itself and insist that all managers do the same for the people in their care.

A close examination of this six-step process reveals that it incorporates the major dimensions as promised. Strategic contingency theory informs the first step, which requires the leader to be both vigilant and proactive in fitting the strategy and structure of the organization to the demands of the environment. The need for vision and alignment, key elements of transformational leadership, inform the second and third steps in the process. In addition, the first three steps serve to unfreeze the organization, in Lewinian terms, in a natural, non-manipulative way and thus create a natural impetus for movement or change.

Steps four and five capitalize on the momentum from the first three steps and enhance it by empowering joint responsibility and action by organizational members to develop workable plans to achieve the vision. The role of culture as a function of the stage of the organization in its life-cycle informs step four, which acknowledges its pivotal role in guiding the choice of interventions that will fit the nature and needs of the organization at the time. Finally, step six emphasizes the critical need for the leader to act as a supportive coach as well as a developer of individuals, groups, and organizations to ensure the continued growth of the organization and its most valuable resource, its people.

Hopefully these comments on the purpose of each step in the integrated leadership and change management model have helped to clarify what it is and how a leader would apply it in practice. By following these steps, transformational leaders who seek to inspire and invite collaboration can engage the hearts and minds of the members of their organizations and bring about meaningful and lasting organization change.

Conclusion

The purpose of this essay has been to lay the theoretical foundation for the analysis of three cases. To that end, this paper has focused on (a) the principles of modern leadership, management, and organizational change, (b) the role of culture and stage in the life cycle in limiting viable change strategies, and (c) the impact of environmental demands and the need to maintain a good organizational fit on organizational strategy and leadership prerogatives.

References

Amburgey, T. L., & Dacin, T. (1994). As the left foot follows the right? The dynamics of strategic and structural change. *Academy of Management Journal, 37*(6), 1427–1452.

Avolio, B. J., Waldman, D. A., & Yammarino, F. J. (1991). Leading in the 1990's: The four I's of transformational leadership. *Journal of European Industrial Training, 15*(4), 9–16.

Bass, B. M. (1990). From transactional to transformational leadership: Learning to share the vision. *Organizational Dynamics, 18*(3), 19–31.

Bennis, W. (1999). New leadership. *Executive Excellence, 16*(11), 7–8.

Bradford, D. L., & Cohen, A. R. (1984). *Managing for excellence: The guide to developing high performance in contemporary organizations.* New York: John Wiley & Sons.

Burke, W. W. (1982). *Organization development: Principles and practices.* Boston: Little, Brown and Company.

Burke, W. W. (1987). *Organization development: A normative view.* Reading, Massachusetts: Addison-Wesley.

Burns, J. M. (1978). *Leadership.* New York: Harper & Row.

Carl, D. E., & Javidian, M. (2001). Universality of char-
    ismatic leadership: A multi-nation study. *Academy
    of Management Proceedings*, B1–B6.

Dvir, T., Eden, D., Avolio, B. J., & Shamir, B. (2002).
    Impact of transformational leadership on follower
    development and performance: A field experiment.
    Academy of Management Journal, 45(4), 735–744.

Eisenbach, R., Watson, K., & Pillai, R. (1999). Transfor-
    mational leadership in the context of organizational
    change. *Journal of Organizational Change Man-
    agement, 12*(2), 80–89.

House, R. J., & Shamir, B. (1993). Toward the integration
    of transformational, charismatic, and visionary
    theories. In M. M. Chemers & R. Ayman (Eds.),
    *Leadership theory and research: Perspectives and
    directions* (pp. 81–107). San Diego: Academic Press.

Javidian, M., & Waldman, D. A. (2003). Exploring char-
    ismatic leadership in the public sector: Measure-
    ment and consequences. *Public Administration
    Review, 63*(2), 229–242.

Johnson, D. W., & Johnson, R. T. (1989). *Cooperation and
    competition: Theory and research*. Edina, MN: In-
    teraction Book Company.

Jung, D. I., & Avolio, B. J. (2000). Opening the black box:
    An experimental investigation of the mediating ef-
    fects of trust and value congruence on transforma-
    tional and transactional leadership. *Journal of
    Organizational Behavior, 21*(8), 949–964.

Kotter, J. P. (1996). *Leading change*. Boston: Harvard Business School Press.

Lawrence, P. R., & Lorsch, J. W. (1986). *Organization and environment: Managing differentiation and integration*. Boston: Harvard Business School Press.

Lee, J., & Miller, D. (1996). Strategy, environment and performance in two technological contexts: Contingency theory in Korea. *Organization Studies, 17*(5), 729–750.

Maxwell, J. A. (1996). *Qualitative research design: An iterative approach*. Thousand Oaks, CA: Sage Publications.

Miller, C. C., & Cardinal, L. B. (1994). Strategic planning and firm performance: A synthesis of more than two decades of research. *Academy of Management Journal, 37*(6), 1649–1665.

Morrow, A. J. (1969). *The practical theorist: The life and work of Kurt Lewin*. New York: Basic Books.

Parry, K. (2000). Does leadership help the bottom line? *New Zealand Management, 47*(3), 38–41.

Pillai, R., & Meindl, J. R. (1991). The effect of crisis on the emergence of charismatic leadership: A laboratory study. *Academy of Management Proceedings*, 235–239.

Schein, E. H. (1992). *Organizational culture and leader-ship* (2nd ed.). San Francisco: Jossey-Bass Publish-ers.

Schein, E. H. (1999). Kurt Lewin's change theory in the field and in the classroom: Notes toward a model of managed learning. *Reflections: The SOL Journal, 1*(1), 59–74.

Scott, W. R. (1998). *Organizations: Rational, natural, and open systems* (4th ed.). Upper Saddle River, NJ: Prentice Hall.

Senge, P. M. (1990). *The fifth discipline: The art and practice of the learning organization.* New York: Doubleday.

Yin, R. K. (2003). *Case study research: Design and meth-ods* (3rd ed.). Thousand Oaks, CA: Sage Publica-tions.

About the Author

Robert E. Levasseur, Ph.D., a full-time faculty member at one of America's premier online Ph.D. granting universities, teaches doctoral courses and mentors Ph.D. students in Leadership and Organizational Change, Information Systems Management, Operations Research, Engineering Management, Accounting, and Knowledge Management.

Dr. Levasseur earned undergraduate degrees in physics and electrical engineering from Bowdoin College and MIT, and master's degrees in electrical engineering and management from Northeastern University and the MIT Sloan School of Management. His Ph.D. is from Walden University.

Dr. Levasseur has taught for Boston University, Anne Arundel Community College, and the University of Maryland University College part-time; and for the University of the Virgin Islands and Walden University full-time.

Dr. Levasseur's professional career spans over three decades and includes leadership, management, and organizational change positions in Fortune 50 corporations. He is a registered Organization Development consultant and a member of INFORMS, the Institute for Operations Research and the Management Sciences.

Dr. Levasseur is the author of numerous articles and books. These include *Breakthrough Business Meetings,*

*Leadership and Change in the 21ˢᵗ Century, Practical
Statistics,* and *Student to Scholar.*

A native of Sanford, Maine, Dr. Levasseur and his wife
live on the shores of the Chesapeake Bay in Annapolis,
Maryland. To learn more about "Dr. L" and his work,
visit his web site at www.mindfirepress.com.